St Magnus Way

Walk or cycle Orkney Mainland

David Mazza

Rucksack Readers

St Magnus Way

First published 2023 by
Rucksack Readers, 6 Old Church Lane, Edinburgh, EH15 3PX, UK

Phone   0131 661 0262 (+44 131 661 0262)
Email: *info@rucsacs.com*
Website   *www.rucsacs.com*

Text, design and mapping are copyright Rucksack Readers © 2023; photos are copyright Rucksack Readers and licensors: see page 71 for credits.

The right of David Mazza to be identified as the author of this work has been asserted by him in accordance with the Copyright, Designs and Patents Act 1988.

All rights reserved. No part of this publication may be reproduced, stored in a retrieval system, or transmitted in any form or by any means, electronic, mechanical, photocopying, recording or otherwise, without prior permission in writing from the publisher and copyright holders.

ISBN 978-1-913817-10-7

British Library cataloguing in publication data: a catalogue record for this book is available from the British Library.

Designed in Scotland by Ian Clydesdale: *ian@clydesdale.scot*

Printed on rainproof, biodegradable paper in the Czech Republic via Akcent Media of St Neots, UK

The mapping in this book is © Rucksack Readers, commissioned from Lovell Johns Ltd: *www.lovelljohns.com*. The mapping contains Ordnance Survey data © Crown copyright and database right 2022-23.

Publisher's note

All information was checked prior to publication. However, changes are inevitable: take local advice and look out for waymarkers and other signage e.g. for diversions. Find out tide times before walking sections 3·2 and 3·6: see page 70. Before setting out, check the official website for updates and advice:
   www.stmagnusway.com
Parts of the Way may be wet underfoot, others are exposed and remote, and the weather in Orkney is unpredictable year-round. Take extra care on clifftop sections, especially in windy weather and poor visibility. You are responsible for your own safety, and for ensuring that your clothing and supplies are suited to your needs. The publisher cannot accept any liability for any ill-health, accident or loss arising directly or indirectly from reading this book.

Feedback is welcome and will be rewarded: email *info@rucsacs.com*

We thank all readers for any comments and suggestions. All feedback will be followed up, and readers whose comments lead to changes will be entitled to claim a free copy of our next edition upon publication. Please email us at *info@rucsacs.com*.

Contents

	Foreword by Magnus Linklater	4
1	**Planning to walk the Way**	5
	Themes of the St Magnus Way	5
	Destination Orkney	6
	Best time of year and weather	8
	How long will it take?	8
	Walk, cycle or both?	9
	Accommodation and refreshments	9
	Getting there and away	11
	Times and tides	11
	Navigation and waymarking	12
	Terrain and gradients	12
	Responsible access	14
	Livestock, walkers and dogs	14
	Packing checklist	15
2	**Background information**	
	2·1 History	16
	2·2 St Magnus and his cathedral	20
	2·3 Geology and scenery	23
	2·4 Habitats and wildlife	25
3	**The Way in detail**	
	3·1 Egilsay	30
	3·2 Gurness to Birsay	33
	3·3 Birsay to Dounby	41
	3·4 Dounby to Finstown	46
	3·5 Finstown to Orphir	52
	3·6 Orphir to Kirkwall	58
	Kirkwall	66
4	**St Magnus Cycleway**	68
5	**Reference**	
	Cathedral, museums, weather and tides	70
	Maps, accommodation and other links	70
	Travel and transport, Notes for novices and credits	71
	Index	72

Foreword

My earliest memory of Orkney is standing outside the house where I was born. I was four years old. My back was to the Harray Loch, and I was looking up at white clouds scudding across a sky of the brightest blue. I turned towards the house – Merkister – and, as the clouds flew high over the roof, the house suddenly looked as if it was falling forwards on top of me. In terror I turned and ran straight into the stone wall behind me. The scar on my forehead is with me still.

So too is the lure of Orkney, whose hallmark is wide open sky. Each time we come back, it casts the same spell – that of homecoming. Clouded sky above, green fields beneath, and the horizon stretching as far as you can see. For anyone following the St Magnus Way, that will be an abiding image. Because the land is rolling – not exactly flat, but never mountainous – you are always aware of the sky's dome above you. That, and the sea of course.

Most of those who arrive in Orkney to make the St Magnus pilgrimage will come by boat, arriving in Stromness, which my father described as a town that tumbles into the sea. It is the place where the great poet George Mackay Brown lived, and from which he took his inspiration. He wrote of the sea when it is storm-driven as something 'treacherous, which … took more than ever it gave'. But he also loved it at peace, stretching calm beyond the green fields: 'blue hand and green hand together, like praying, in the summer dawn'.

Orkney is a rich land that has drawn settlers over many thousands of years. Their legacy is everywhere – in standing stones, tombs, and dwellings. The martyrdom of St Magnus on Egilsay is one of its darker episodes. However, it led to the glory of St Magnus Cathedral, built in homage to the martyred saint. In his *Songs for St Magnus Day*, Mackay Brown wrote: 'Saint Magnus, keep for us a jar of light, beyond sun and star'. He has left more than a jar – he leaves the Orkney sky, which, for all those who travel it, will light the St Magnus Way.

Magnus Linklater CBE

1 Planning to walk the Way

The St Magnus Way is a challenging and rewarding 60-mile (96-km) walk through the beautiful landscape of Orkney. It was created in 2017 to commemorate the 900th anniversary of the death of St Magnus of Orkney and to encourage exploration of the physical and spiritual heritage of Orkney. It follows a well waymarked route around Orkney Mainland in five sections. These are preceded by an excursion by ferry to the small island of Egilsay to visit the site of St Magnus' martyrdom. For the creation of the route, see page 70.

On Mainland, the route follows the traditional journey of Magnus' body from the coast of Evie to Christ's Kirk in Birsay where he was originally buried. The route continues south from Birsay to the shores of Scapa Flow. It culminates at the impressive St Magnus Cathedral, Kirkwall, founded in 1137 to house his remains.

Themes of the St Magnus Way

St Magnus Way incorporates pilgrimage sites and routes to encourage walkers to consider themselves as pilgrims. A different theme is associated with each part of the route. The island of Egilsay marks the place where Magnus was martyred. The theme of Peace encourages thinking about the sacrifice that he made there for the sake of peace in Orkney, and our continuing need for peace in the midst of conflict.

As the journey continues, the five Mainland sections focus on themes of Loss, Growth, Change, Forgiveness and Hospitality. These themes and their associated questions can stimulate reflection as part of the process of walking through the glorious Orkney landscape. These texts are linked from *www.rucsacs.com/books/smw* and also reproduced on the prayer paddles in St Magnus Cathedral.

St Magnus Church, Egilsay

Destination Orkney

Orkney is an archipelago of 70 islands of which 20 are inhabited. At its closest point, it lies only 6 miles off the north-east coast of Scotland (Duncansby Head), but the island group measures over 50 miles across. Its population is about 22,000 people, of whom nearly half live in its two largest settlements, the capital Kirkwall (8500) and the town of Stromness (2200). It has been voted 'Scotland's best place to live' for eight years in succession, according to a Bank of Scotland survey. And as a place where you are never more than a few miles from the sea, its maritime tradition, astonishing coastline and natural harbour of Scapa Flow are huge influences on life in Orkney.

For up to 9000 years, Orkney's fertile terrain and easy access by sea has made it attractive to settlers. It boasts some of the most important Neolithic sites in western Europe, dating from about 3000 BC. These include the settlement of Skara Brae, the great chambered tomb of Maeshowe and two impressive stone circles with henges – the Stones of Stenness and Ring of Brodgar. Together these four comprise UNESCO's Heart of Neolithic Orkney World Heritage Site (inscribed in 1999): see page 16.

Skipping forward to the late 8th century, Orkney was settled by people from what is now Norway and ruled by earls under Norwegian sovereignty until 1472. Magnus, later Saint Magnus, at first shared the earldom of Orkney with his cousin Håkon. The story of their deadly power struggle and Magnus' martyrdom in about 1116 is told in part 2·1.

Orkney has been part of Scotland only since February 1472 when, like Shetland, it formed part of the dowry of Margaret of Denmark, daughter of Christian I of Norway. In 1469, at the age of 13, she married King James III of Scotland. Later, the union of the Scottish and English crowns (1603) and Parliaments (1707) made Orkney part of what became the United Kingdom.

Any visit to Orkney offers an experience of a unique culture, with distinctive history and Norse heritage evident in its placenames and everyday language. From the 8th and 9th centuries AD, Norwegian settlers named the places in Orkney, drawing from their language Norn (derived from Old Norse). Norn was spoken until the early 15th century when its gradual replacement by the English language accelerated. The last speaker of Norn died as recently as 1850.

Although many Norse names have become anglicised, often that affects their spelling more than their pronunciation. Placenames ending in -**say** are pronounced more like -**sea** or -**see** e.g. Egilsay sounds more like **Egilsea**.

Since many Orkney words are new to visitors from mainland Britain, let alone from further afield, we have listed some useful ones including prefixes and suffixes. For convenience, the table shows only the most common examples, and includes a few that are not of Norn origin.

word or part of word	meaning
-**bigging**	building
-**bister**, -**buster**	farm, dwelling
breck	slope
broch	Iron Age round stone tower
bu, by	farm
-**dale**, -**dall**	valley
firth, -**ford**	fjord, bay
geo	ravine
holm	small island
howe	mound
kir-, kirk-	church (also corn)
knowe	knoll, mound
ling	heather
-**ness**	point, headland
noust	place to haul out a boat
peerie, peedie	small
-**quoy**	cattle pen
sten-, -stain	stone
strom	tide, stream
ting	assembly
-**ton, -town**	enclosure
voe, -wall, wick	bay

In summary, Orkney has a wide range of attractions as a destination: in addition to its world-class prehistory and distinctive heritage, it has extraordinary wildlife, especially seabirds: see pages 25 to 29. At a practical level, walkers will relish its delicious dairy products, meat and seafood; and they may enjoy tasting products from its breweries and whisky and gin distilleries. Above all, Orcadians offer a special brand of welcoming hospitality. So we recommend anyone who intends to walk the Way to plan some extra days, not only to explore other sites on Orkney Mainland, but also to visit some of its islands.

Best time of year and weather

Most people will opt to walk St Magnus Way in late spring, summer or early autumn. Wildflowers are at their best in late spring and summer, and birds are more active and visible during early spring and autumn. Accommodation will also be more limited out of season, so the best months overall are from April to October.

In theory, the Way could be walked at any time of year. It never involves high altitude and the major constraints on winter walking are short days, greater chance of wet, windy weather and sodden ground in the offroad sections. Unless you live at high latitude (about 59° N) you may not realise how much the hours of daylight vary – from over 18 hours in late June to barely six hours in late December.

Whatever the season in Orkney, it is rare to have a week of uninterrupted wind and rain, but it is also unusual for settled weather to last more than a few days. It's usually likely to be windy, and in summer this makes sun protection extra important: it's easy to forget how strongly the sun burns. Any hat needs a strap or lanyard or it may blow away.

Finally, be aware that Orkney is prone to sea fog (aka *haar*), especially in summer months. It forms when warm moist air is chilled by the sea, causing condensation. Unless the land is warm and the sunshine strong, the fog may take a long time to burn off, especially if a sea breeze keeps sweeping more fog inland. It is not only damp and cooling, but also reduces visibility drastically; this can make navigation challenging.

How long will it take?

Your ideal itinerary depends on your preferred pace and fitness, and, perhaps crucially, on the availability of accommodation in key places. The route is intended as a long and enjoyable walk, not as a test of endurance or speed. Most walkers will need six days for the entire route.

This book presents the walk in six sections, and we hope you will be inspired to complete the whole itinerary. However, we recognise that some readers will have limited time in Orkney, that some may have to compromise with non-walking friends and family and that readers' priorities and preferences vary. We therefore suggest some possible variations.

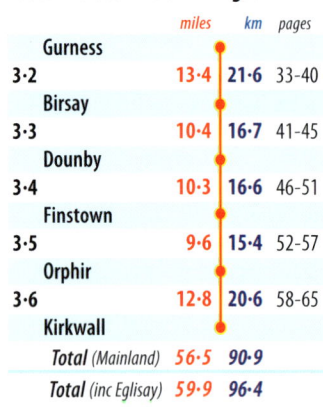

Table 1 Distances and stages

		miles	km	pages
	Gurness			
3.2		13.4	21.6	33-40
	Birsay			
3.3		10.4	16.7	41-45
	Dounby			
3.4		10.3	16.6	46-51
	Finstown			
3.5		9.6	15.4	52-57
	Orphir			
3.6		12.8	20.6	58-65
	Kirkwall			
	Total (Mainland)	56.5	90.9	
	Total (inc Eglisay)	59.9	96.4	

If you have only five days to spare, the most obvious way to save a day is to omit Egilsay, which simplifies the public transport (buses and ferries). This comes at a price: you would miss the whole island experience – not only the site of Magnus' martyrdom, but also the golden sandy beaches of the east coast and the RSPB Onziebust nature reserve. For the fit and ambitious walker, another five-day option is to retain Egilsay but combine sections 3.3

and 3·4 so as to walk from Birsay direct to Finstown. This makes a very long day, but the terrain is not challenging and you save a mile by bypassing Dounby. If you are not fazed by the idea of a 19·7-mile day then the long hours of summer daylight certainly make it possible.

Another option for saving a day may appeal to those who dislike road walking. From Dounby to Finstown the Way runs 75% on tarmac, and you could skip this section making use of the Stagecoach bus service.

If you are new to long-distance walking, St Magnus Way is a good choice provided you take heed of weather and tide warnings. You are advised to obtain our *Notes for novices*: see page 71.

Walk, cycle or both?

A more radical choice is whether to walk or cycle, or even perhaps to mix the two. The 67-mile St Magnus Cycleway connects the same places as the walkers' mainland route, but it follows tarmac roads almost throughout: see pages 68-9 for a map and more information. The mileages shown there are measured from Kirkwall, following the direction indicated on the website. However you could reverse the direction if you prefer.

It can be completed in a single day by the experienced, fit cyclist or enjoyed in a more leisurely way as either or both of two circuits: a 27-mile southern loop from Kirkwall and/or a 40-mile northern circuit from Finstown. And if you can sort out the logistics, you could even cycle part of the route and walk the rest, bearing in mind that as of 2022 the only bike shop in Orkney is in Kirkwall: visit *www.cycleorkney.com*.

Accommodation and refreshments

There is a range of hotels, bed and breakfasts, self-catering cottages and campsites in Orkney although it can be hard to find accommodation for a single night: some B&Bs and nearly all self-catering require minimum stays from two nights and upward. Popular locations can become fully booked months in advance, often by people who return to Orkney every year.

One option is to stay in the same accommodation for several nights or even for the whole week and arrange with the owner, or with a taxi company, dropoffs and pickups at beginning and end of each section of the Way. The taxi option is more affordable if you have a group of at least four walkers.

With advance planning and a flexible attitude and budget, you may be able to book accommodation at the end of each section. The official website suggests

Table 2 Accommodation and refreshments

	B&B/hotel*	hostel/bunkhouse	pub/café*	shop	campsite	public toilet
Evie (1·6 miles offroute)				✓		✓
Birsay	✓	✓	✓	✓	✓	✓
Dounby	✓		✓	✓		✓
Finstown	✓		✓	✓		✓
Orphir	✓					✓
Kirkwall	✓	✓	✓	✓	✓	✓

* not necessarily serving food in the evening

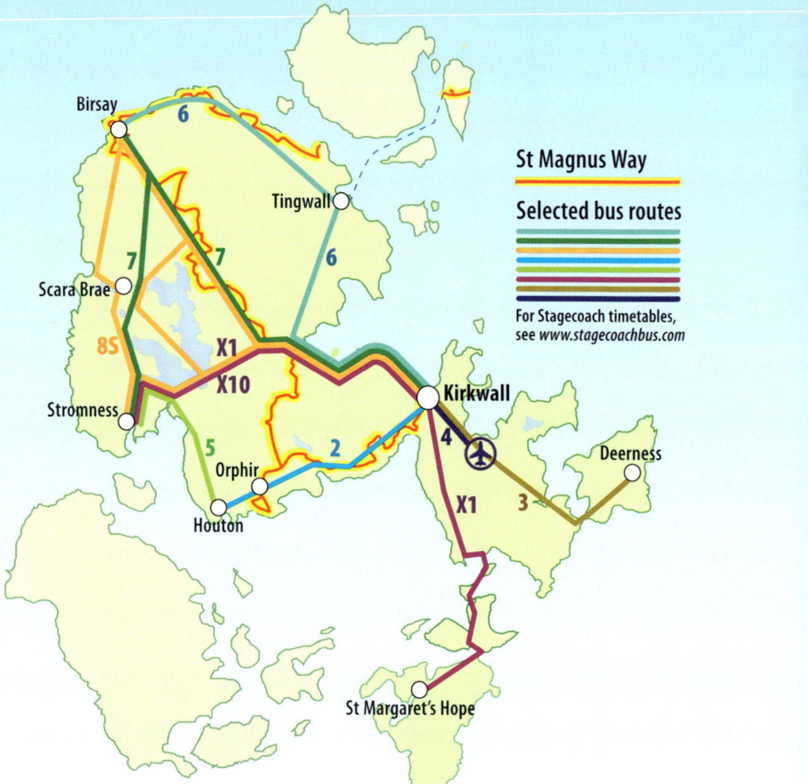

accommodation options on that basis: see *bit.ly/SMW-accomm*. Currently you cannot overnight on Egilsay unless you wild camp. This is camping by small numbers for up to 2-3 nights and it is legal in Scotland provided that it is done responsibly: see the panel about SOAC on page 14. Avoid camping in enclosed fields of crops or among livestock, and if you want to camp near a building, seek permission from the owner. There are spaces suitable for wild camping at the end of every section of the Way, although privacy may be limited by the open nature of the landscape.

There are limited local bus services connecting with the beginning and end of each section. Before relying on them, check timetables carefully: see page 71.

The locations of shops selling food are marked on the maps and listed in the facilities table. Be prepared to plan in advance what food supplies to carry: only Birsay, Dounby and Finstown have conveniently located shops. As of 2022, at section-ends, only Dounby and Kirkwall have pubs or restaurants that offer evening meals. However, some B&B hosts may be able to help if you shop for supplies. Always carry plenty of drinking water for the day's walk, unless you rely on purifying tablets or filters.

Wild camping on the beach near Gurness

Getting there and away

Orkney is well connected with mainland Scotland and the rest of the UK, with plenty of travel options.

By air: flights to Kirkwall (KOI) are operated by Loganair from Glasgow, Edinburgh, Inverness, Aberdeen, Shetland and London. There are two or three flights a day arriving in Kirkwall seven days a week: see page 71.

By sea: choose from three main vehicle ferry routes. NorthLink Ferries has sailings from Aberdeen to Kirkwall and from Scrabster to Stromness, and Pentland Ferries plies between Gills Bay and South Ronaldsay. For details of duration, links to timetables and a further seasonal option, see page 71.

By bus: Stagecoach buses run to Aberdeen, Thurso and Gills Bay, with ongoing ferry connections to Orkney: see page 71.

By train: Rail services to Aberdeen and Thurso are operated by Scotrail. Aberdeen railway station is a ten-minute walk from the ferry terminal. Thurso railway station is two miles away from the ferry port at Scrabster. For ferry connections there is a restricted Stagecoach bus service, or you may prefer to book taxi travel, bearing in mind minimum check-in times (which are longer if taking a vehicle).

Times and tides

Certain sections of the Way may be difficult or impassable around high tide. This applies particularly to the first couple of miles from the Broch of Gurness, and at Waulkmill Bay. In both cases, alternative routes are described: see pages 34-5 and 58-9. The optional detour to the Brough of Birsay (a tidal island) involves crossing a causeway: read page 39 carefully before deciding when to set off.

There are normally two high tides daily, about 12·5 hours apart, with two low tides in between. Tidal range varies widely, and wind, waves and local landforms all affect the actual level. Be extra cautious in extreme weather and at certain times in the lunar month. High tides are highest (and low tides lowest) just after full moon and new moon, especially around the equinoxes (late March and late September).

In tide tables, heights are predictions, normally in metres, but check if the time is in Greenwich Mean Time; if so, add one hour whenever British Summer Time is in force. Retail outlets and information centres may display tide times locally, but if you want to plan ahead, refer to the sources on page 70.

Navigation and waymarking

The mapping in Part 3 is detailed and closely linked with the route description: if you follow directions carefully, navigation should be straightforward. Note that each page carries a km grid in pale grey, and the route line has mileage indicators that are cumulative from the Broch of Gurness. Your mileage on Egilsay is additional to the walk on Mainland.

The route is well waymarked, usually with a black and white logo, sometimes supported by a direction arrow below. This waymarker logo is a monochrome version of the full colour logo's upper half. It may be found on timber posts, concrete fence supports or on natural stones or trees. At present, the waymarking is in one direction only, from Gurness to Kirkwall, so if you plan to reverse any part of the route you may need to look at the back of the post or support. The cycleway is not waymarked at all, so you need to refer to the mapping: see page 68.

Terrain and gradients

The St Magnus Way runs over a wide variety of surfaces, ranging from clifftop paths and sandy beaches through moorland footpaths and farm tracks to tarmac roads and pavements. The photos above give some idea of the range of surfaces, but be aware that rainfall (before and around the time that you walk) also affects terrain. Most of the paths are fairly well-drained, but your

footwear still needs to be waterproof for walking in the rain and through long wet vegetation.

The route is generally low-level, reaching its highest point of 165 m on the Hill of Lyradale in section 3.5. Don't assume that this makes for easy walking. Some of the coastal walking in sections 3·2 and 3·6 is demanding because of broken ground, boulders and concealed hazards – none of it daunting for those used to offroad walking, but taking care makes for slow going. Section 3·1 is a standalone excursion by ferry with a short but rewarding walk on a scenic island.

There are sections of coastal walk with significant exposure. Be extra careful on windy days when it is vital to keep well away from the cliff edge. The views of the dramatic coastline are exhilarating but if you don't have a head for heights you may find this a challenge, especially where there are geos – narrow clefts formed by the sea's battering of the cliffs.

A significant proportion of the St Magnus Way runs along roads of various kinds. Whilst traffic is limited in Orkney, vehicles can still legally be travelling at up to 60 mph in places. Where there is no pavement or walkable verge, always walk on the right to face oncoming traffic and be alert for traffic in both directions. When approaching sharp bends, be aware of drivers' sight lines and adjust your position if need be. Drivers in Orkney are used to pedestrians on the road and will usually give them a wide berth, but you must be ready to step off the road when necessary. When drivers give you space, do acknowledge their courtesy with a wave or a smile.

Enjoy Scotland's outdoors responsibly

Everyone has the right to be on most land and inland water providing they act responsibly. Your access rights and responsibilities are explained fully in the Scottish Outdoor Access Code.

Whether you're in the outdoors or managing the outdoors, the key things are to:

- take responsibility for your own actions
- respect the interests of other people
- care for the environment.

Visit **outdooraccess-scotland.scot** for full details. See also page ??.

KNOW THE CODE BEFORE YOU GO
outdooraccess-scotland.scot

Responsible access

Access rights for walkers, cyclists and equestrians are extensive in Scotland. The Scottish Outdoor Access Code spells out how everybody has the statutory right to take access to land, including that which is privately owned, for recreational purposes – provided only that those rights are exercised responsibly.

There are of course some exceptions, such as gardens, farmyards and fields under cultivation; however, landowners are encouraged to provide viable paths around field edges. See the panel for further details of the Code and how to download practical guidance for walkers and cyclists.

As explained, wild camping is allowed under SOAC provided it is done responsibly, but if you prefer campsites with facilities then refer to our table/mapping.

Livestock, walkers and dogs

Much of the St Magnus Way runs adjacent to farmland with livestock and crosses some sheep and cattle fields. If you walk with a dog, it must be under close control, and preferably on a lead. During lambing time (between March and June) your dog will be unwelcome in any fields with sheep. During the same season birds may be nesting on the ground, and again dogs must be under very close control. See the panel about SOAC above.

Packing checklist

What you need to bring with you depends both on your personal needs and also on your itinerary and the season and likely weather. If you have any access to a support vehicle or baggage transfer, you may be able to carry few overnight things, or even none. If you are carrying everything for yourself, be aware that every kilogram counts. A heavy rucksack will not only make harder work out of stiles and steep slopes, but also will compromise your balance on exposed clifftops. Travel light and enjoy the walk.

The official website and app provide helpful guidance and background information on the route: see *www.stmagnusway.com*. Note that mobile phone (cellphone) coverage is patchy on the Way and should not be relied on for navigation or for emergencies.

Experienced walkers will already know what they habitually need, and may differ about what is essential and desirable. Newcomers may find the following checklist helpful:

Essential
- rucksack (e.g 25-35 litres)
- waterproof rucksack cover or liner(s)
- comfortable walking boots and/or shoes
- specialist walking socks
- waterproof jacket and overtrousers
- clothing in layers (tops, trousers, jacket)
- hats for warmth and sun protection
- gloves
- guidebook with maps
- water carrier and plenty of water
- food for the more remote sections
- first aid kit, including blister treatment
- toilet tissue (biodegradable)
- overnight kit including toiletries
- insect repellent, sun protection (summer)

Desirable
- walking poles
- spare socks
- gaiters
- plastic bag(s) for litter
- camera and spare memory card
- spare batteries or charger for camera
- binoculars (useful for wildlife)
- notebook and pen
- pouch or secure pockets for keeping small items handy and safe
- mobile phone.

For campers
The above list assumes that you are using B&Bs. If you are camping, you'll also need a tent, sleeping gear, cooking utensils, portable stove, fuel and food, and a much larger rucksack to carry it all.

East over Bay of Firth

2·1 History

The first settlers in Orkney arrived over 8000 years ago, possibly from Doggerland, the land bridge between Britain and the rest of Europe; they were hunter-gatherers. Up to 3000 years later, settlers arrived from what is now France. They built many remarkable structures that predate Stonehenge and survive almost intact.

Some are scattered throughout Orkney, but four on the Mainland comprise the Heart of Neolithic Orkney World Heritage Site: the settlement of Skara Brae, the chambered tomb of Maeshowe and two huge stone circles – the Stones of Stenness and Ring of Brodgar. In 2002, a massive complex of neolithic buildings was found at the Ness of Brodgar and its excavation continues, shedding new light on this period.

Standing stones of Stenness

Neolithic people brought with them domesticated animals and cereals, particularly *bere*, a primitive form of barley still grown and milled in Orkney at Barony Mill: see page 41. They made skilful use of the local flagstone for building. Dating from 3600 BC, the Knap of Howar on Papa Westray is the oldest stone house in northern Europe. Work began on the complex of houses at Skara Brae in Orkney Mainland around 3100 BC so these houses are older than Egypt's pyramids.

The impressive standing stones of Stenness were also erected in about 3100 BC and the Ring of Brodgar followed some 600 years later. The collaboration and effort required to plan and construct these suggest that the population was thriving, with ample access to food and fuel. They made fine, decorated pottery (now known as Unstan Ware and Grooved Ware), painted walls with natural pigments and carved patterns into stone. The houses at Skara Brae are strikingly similar to each other, with no obvious variation in status, perhaps suggesting a relatively egalitarian society.

Skara Brae

Ring of Brodgar

The archaeological record becomes more limited for the Bronze Age period from about 2000 to 500 BC when it seems the climate changed, becoming colder and wetter. Failing crops and overpopulation seem to have led to some emigration. During the Iron Age (500 BC to 800 AD), communities were organised into fortified settlements with a ruling class. A new Iron Age structure emerged – the broch – a double-walled circular stone structure that was easy to defend. The Broch of Gurness is a striking example: see page 33. The Way passes the remains of another five brochs on the northern coast, with a further six on Rousay facing them across Eynhallow Sound.

By the 4th century AD, the Picts had developed from Iron Age Celtic tribes across Scotland, including Orkney, and formed local federations each with its own leader. By the 7th century, perhaps earlier, Irish monks from western Scotland and Ireland had brought Christianity to Orkney. Pictish cross slabs show Orkney's religious connections to Pictland in the 8th century, a time when settlement was dispersed in family farmsteads.

The influence of Vikings from Norway began in the 9th century and Orkney was part of Norway until the 15th century. With sheltered harbours, fertile land and productive seas, and only a few days' sailing from Norway, Orkney was an important staging post for Scandinavian expeditions to Britain.

There is no evidence here of the pillaging, destruction or burning typically associated with Viking invasion, and perhaps the Norse travellers settled alongside the inhabitants, introducing their own distinctive culture. Whether the process of assimilation was natural or forced, Orkney became demonstrably Norse. Recent genetic studies show that many of today's Orcadians are related to early Norse settlers and they take great pride in their Norse ancestry. Fresh discoveries continue to shed light on the Norse period, including the Viking boat burial found in Scar, Sanday in 1985 – the source of this whale-bone plaque.

The Norse earls ruled Orkney from the 11th to the 13th century and this period is colourfully described in the Orkneyinga Saga: see page 71. The earldom was subject to the Norwegian king and benefitted from Orkney's strategic position between Scandinavia and Britain. The earl's rule reached beyond Orkney, with Earl Thorfinn Sigurdsson (Thorfinn the Mighty) extending his authority from his Birsay base to Caithness, Sutherland and the Hebrides. He appointed the first bishop of Orkney and built the Christchurch, the remains of which may lie under St Magnus' Church in Birsay. This church became the first consecrated burial site of Thorfinn's grandson, Magnus Erlendsson. The story of his martyrdom and canonisation is told on pages 20-22.

When Magnus' nephew, Rognvald Kolsson became earl in 1135, he moved the seat of power in Orkney from Birsay to Kirkwall. In 1137 Rognvald started to build a cathedral to house Magnus' remains and to promote the cult associated with Magnus. Rognvald was murdered in 1158 and, like Magnus, buried in the cathedral. Later he was also canonised after miracles allegedly took place at his grave.

While acknowledging Norwegian sovereignty, the earls of Orkney were becoming increasingly integrated into the Scottish aristocracy through marriage and birth. The last Norse earl was murdered in 1231 and died without an heir. Afterwards the earldom passed into the Scottish aristocracy – namely the Earls of Angus and later the St Clair's from Midlothian.

Orkney was officially handed over to Scotland in 1472 as part of a dowry: see page 7. Scottish influence on Orkney's customs, language and society continued, with the migration of increasing numbers of Scots. Whilst Orkney in the 16th and 17th century was a place of opportunity for Scottish aristocrats, periods of famine and plague made this a brutal period for ordinary Orcadians. The tyranny of some earls, notably Robert Stewart and his son Patrick, added to the misery of the population. The architectural ambition of the Stewart earls can be seen in the ruins of their palaces in Birsay and in Kirkwall: see pages 41 and 67.

Conditions for Orcadians slowly improved during the 18th and 19th centuries, when resident lairds owned and managed the land. In the 18th century, Orkney became the centre of the kelp industry, with shallow waters and sloping beaches making collection possible. Kelp was harvested and burned to extract potash and soda, used as a fertiliser and in glass and soap production. At its peak (1789-1830) Orkney exported 3000 tons of kelp per annum.

John Rae's memorial, St Magnus Cathedral

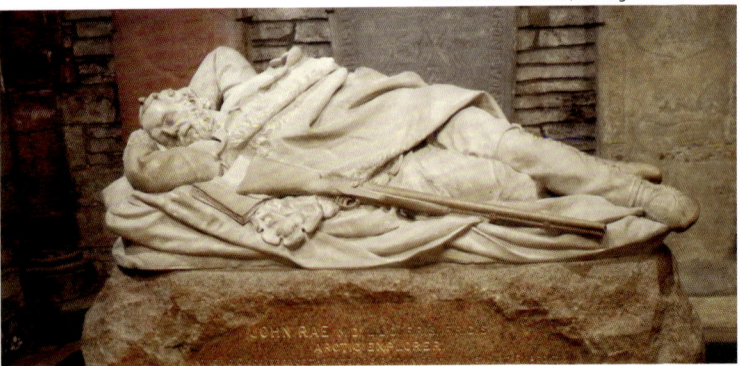

The Italian Chapel, Lamb Holm

During this period, large numbers of Orcadians were employed by the Hudson's Bay Company, involved in transatlantic trade and exploration. Outstanding among these was John Rae (1813-93) who discovered the final portion of the Northwest Passage in Canada in 1854. A man of extraordinary stamina, skills in boat-handling and an expert in living off the land, his reputation has been restored only recently: see page 70.

Many Orkney men provided crews for the increasing numbers of whaling ships. As a result of such maritime activity, Stromness grew rapidly to become Orkney's second largest town, and Kirkwall's harbour was enlarged.

In the 20th century, the sheltered anchorage of Scapa Flow became the base for the British navy's battle fleet during World Wars 1 and 2: see the panel on page 62. At its peak in World War 1, the garrison in Orkney stood at 100,000 personnel. Reminders of this period are still widespread, including gun emplacements, pillboxes and concrete foundations. Many old military buildings have been adapted for farm or domestic use.

A famous survivor from World War 2 is the Italian Chapel in Lamb Holm. It was created and decorated by Italian prisoners of war based in Orkney to construct the Churchill Barriers. Churchill commissioned these causeways after the sinking of HMS Royal Oak by a German submarine in 1939. The Scapa Flow Museum in Lyness, Hoy, tells the story of wartime Orkney: see page 70.

Churchill barrier 1 linking Mainland with Lamb Holm

2·2 Magnus and his cathedral

Much of what is known about St Magnus comes from the Orkneyinga Saga, a collection of stories written in Iceland in the 13th century by unknown authors. Combining historic with fictionalised accounts, it tells the story of the conquest of Orkney by Norway and of notable Norse Earls.

Magnus Erlendsson was born in Orkney about 1080. His father Erlend and uncle Paul shared the earldom of Orkney until the King of Norway, Magnus Barelegs, invaded Orkney and installed his son Sigurd as earl. The King then took Magnus and his cousin, Håkon (Paul's son) on a raiding trip down the west coast of the British Isles. During a battle in Anglesey, Magnus refused to fight and sang psalms instead, saying to the King that he didn't have anything against the people there.

Magnus subsequently escaped and lived in Scotland, England and Wales until he returned to Orkney to share the earldom with his cousin, Håkon. He married Ingarth, a Scottish noblewoman. The couple had no children and, according to legend, Magnus had a cold bath whenever there was a risk that physical desire would get the better of him. This story may have grown up to amplify Magnus' saintliness.

The power sharing arrangement in Orkney proved to be increasingly difficult. Magnus was a popular ruler and his popularity made Håkon jealous. A battle between the two sides at the place of assembly (probably Tingwall) was averted by agreement to have a meeting to resolve their differences on the island of Egilsay on 16 April 1116 (or possibly 1117). Egilsay was probably considered to be neutral territory because it belonged to the Bishop.

Magnus arrived in Egilsay with the agreed two ships and a small number of men. When he saw Håkon arriving with eight ships he realised that Håkon had betrayed him and he went to the church to pray. Magnus insisted that his men should not defend him as this would lead to the futile loss of their lives, given how greatly they were outnumbered.

Magnus realised that his options were limited. He suggested to Håkon that he could be banished from Orkney or go on pilgrimage to Rome or Jerusalem. Håkon refused to consider these options but did agree to Magnus' suggestion that he be blinded and mutilated thereby removing any future threat. However, the chiefs who supported Håkon demanded that Magnus was killed to avoid any further risk of instability in the earldom.

St Magnus Window, Cathedral North Transept

The Orkneyinga Saga tells us that when Håkon's standard bearer Ofeig refused to perform the execution, instead Håkon ordered his cook Lifolf to kill Magnus. The distressed cook was comforted by the condemned man, who said 'Don't be afraid, you're doing this against your will and the man who gives you the order is a greater sinner than you are'. Magnus then took time to pray for those who were about to kill him and forgave them for their crime. As a chieftain, rather than a common thief, he asked Lifolf to strike his head rather than behead him. Before the fatal blow, Magnus reassured his executioner: 'take heart, poor fellow, I've prayed that God grant you his mercy'.

At first, Håkon refused Magnus a Christian burial and he was left where he was slain on Egilsay: see page 32. Later, at his mother Thora's request he was interred in Christchurch in Birsay, built c. 1064 by Earl Thorfinn. The Way visits Birsay, albeit the St Magnus Church that you will see there dates from the 17th to 19th centuries. It stands on one of the possible sites of the original Christchurch and has notable stained glass, including the vestibule window below, by Orcadian artist Shona McInnes (installed in 2013).

Very soon after his death, word began to spread of miracles and healing associated with Magnus and he was made a saint, and his remains enshrined, probably in 1137. As Kirkwall became the centre of power in Orkney, Magnus' relics were moved from Birsay to St Olaf's Church in Kirkwall. Finally he was laid to rest in St Magnus Cathedral when it was consecrated in the 1150s.

The Way largely follows the traditional route taken by those carrying Magnus – from near Gurness, where his body was brought ashore after travelling by sea from Egilsay, to Birsay and then on to Kirkwall. A number of stones known as Mans Stones or Mansie Stanes are said to have been used as resting places for the coffin and shrine during this journey. Some were blessed and considered sacred because of their association with St Magnus. The only remaining Mans Stone is at Strathyre: see page 43.

St Magnus Cathedral was founded in 1137 by Earl Rognvald, Magnus' nephew. Masons who had worked on the cathedrals at Durham and Dunfermline used local red and fawn sandstone in combination to create the fine Romanesque building which dominates the Kirkwall skyline. Before land reclamation, the cathedral originally stood on the shore of the Peedie Sea and would have dominated Kirkwall as seen from

Vestibule window, St Magnus Church, Birsay

the sea. The interior of the cathedral is tranquil, its imposing grandeur balanced by the welcoming warmth of the sandstone.

From the time of its consecration, the shrine of St Magnus was an important place of pilgrimage. A tangible link with the Orkneyinga Saga was discovered during renovation work in 1919. Remains were discovered in a pinewood box in a space in the square pillar to the right of the organ. The skull has a cleft in it, consistent with an axe blow, which suggested that the remains were those of Magnus. During earlier Victorian renovations, various carved stone memorials were removed from the floor of the nave. These have well-preserved lettering and striking symbols of death, and now stand against the inside walls of the nave.

St Magnus Cathedral is owned by the people of Orkney and serves as a parish church for the Church of Scotland. It also acts as a focus for the history and cultural life of Orkney, and it includes memorials to notable Orcadians including Edwin Muir, George Mackay Brown, Eric Linklater and John Rae.

The Society of the Friends of St Magnus Cathedral was founded in 1958 and works closely with Orkney Islands Council and the Church of Scotland to fund restoration work. For details, see the excellent guidebook listed on page 71.

In 1987 a stained glass west window by Lanarkshire artist Crear McCartney was installed to commemorate the building's 850th anniversary. This splendid window is best seen in the afternoon or evening when daylight spills its vibrant colours onto the pillars and walls of the nave. Its main theme is the light of God and it features Christian, Norse and Orcadian imagery. At its apex is a dove, a symbol of peace. But behind the dove is an axe which recalls Magnus' violent death.

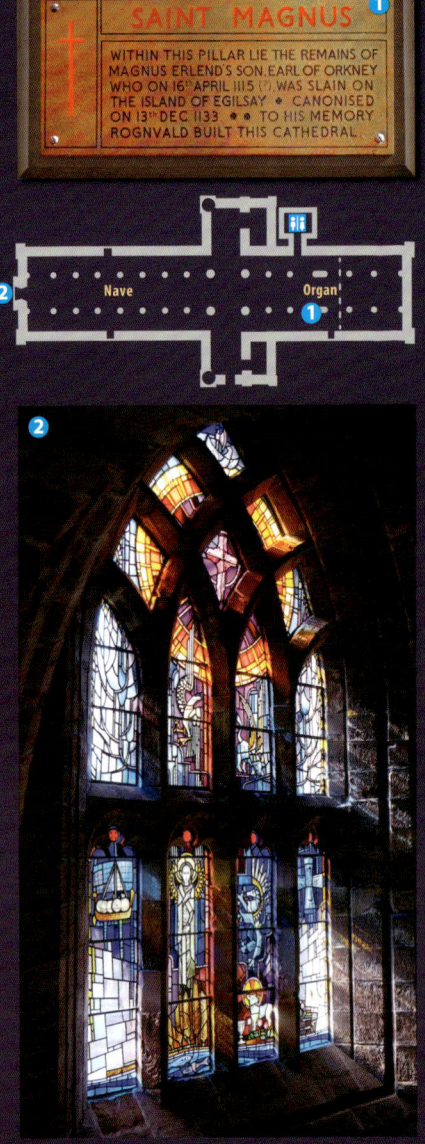

2·3 Geology and scenery

In geological terms, Orkney is an extension of the north-east of Scotland and its sandstone bedrock is known as Caithness flagstone. This is a type of Old Red Sandstone formed in the Devonian period about 400 million years ago. It was created from the mud, sand and fossil beds laid down in the sediment in Lake Orcadie, which at that time was south of the equator, fed by rivers flowing from surrounding mountains.

The subtropical climate affected the depth and size of the lake. Orkney's landscape was formed from layers of sedimentary rock along with much older outcrops of granite, gneiss and schists. Cliffs, rocky shores and exposed inland areas reveal the flagstone's alternating layers of mudstone, coarse siltstone and fine sandstone. The layering means that flagstone readily splits along the line of the bedding. With limited timber, flagstone has been a vital building material in Orkney for thousands of years. Flagstone roofs can still be seen on buildings in Orkney.

Hesta Geo

This landscape has been shaped by heavy glaciation and ice sheets. Successive ice ages have scoured the flagstone to leave smooth rounded hills, sounds and bays. At the end of the last ice age, 13,000 years ago, rising sea levels led to the separation of parts of the land mass to form the many islands of the archipelago.

Glaciation resulted in the formation of Scapa Flow, the largest natural harbour in the northern hemisphere. With a maximum depth of 60 m and a huge expanse of sheltered water, Scapa Flow has been a safe haven since prehistoric times. During World Wars 1 and 2, it was the HQ of the British fleet and one of the most important strategic locations in the world. Its relatively sheltered waters are still important for wildlife. Many birds nest and overwinter here, feeding from the rich waters. The Flow is home to a breeding population of harbour seals and various cetaceans.

Yesnaby cliffs with sea stack (Yesnaby Castle)

Erosion by sea and wind has a continuing impact on the coastal landscape of Orkney. Along some stretches of coast the shore slopes gently into the sea, but on exposed northern and western parts, erosion has created dramatic coastal scenery. Steep cliffs are broken by deep ravines known as *geos*. Sea caves sometimes collapse to form natural arches: a spectacular example is The Gloup in Deerness, where a collapsed cave is separated from the sea by a land bridge.

Perhaps Orkney's most famous landmark is the Old Man of Hoy – at 137 m/450 ft it's Britain's tallest sea stack. Created some time after 1750

Old Man of Hoy

by erosion, it has a worrying crack on top of its south face that may lead to its collapse at any time. Before it's too late, you may wish to spend a day visiting Hoy: ferries go from Stromness or Houton, see page 71. Around Orkney's coastline are many sea stacks, smaller but still impressive, including Yesnaby Castle: see the photo on page 23.

Much of Orkney Mainland consists of fertile farmland. Weathered sandstone combined with glacial clay deposits has created productive soils that support grassland and some cereal production, with peat formation at higher levels. A striking feature of the landscape is the scarcity of larger trees, probably because of exposure to wind and rain, and human activity. The walk through Binscarth Woods is an unexpected pleasure: see page 51.

The rolling, low hills and open landscape of Orkney create expansive views with little to obstruct the distant horizon. The sight and sound of the sea is a constant companion along many parts of the Way. Even where the Way runs inland, water is never far away. The play of light on the lochs in the gentle valleys provides a colourful contrast to the greens and browns of the land. And in the course of the Way, you will enjoy vistas that reveal the hills of Hoy and views over Scapa Flow and the distant Atlantic Ocean.

West towards Marwick from Greeny Hill

2·4 Habitats and wildlife

For the present purpose, Orkney's habitats can be covered under three headings: • coastal   • moorland   • marshes and lochs

Strictly speaking, there are two other kinds of habitat: woodland and maritime heath. Woodland is exceptional in wind-swept Orkney, but the Way passes through Binscarth Woods in a sheltered valley near Finstown: see page 51. Maritime heath is mainly confined to the western side of Rousay. It is a favourite breeding site for the most extreme traveller in the avian world: the arctic tern. They make an annual round trip of some 15,000 miles to Antarctica.

Orkney's wildlife differs from that of mainland Britain. Because there are no foxes, badgers or weasels, many species of ground-nesting birds have been thriving here for centuries. So, major problems have been caused by the recent arrival of the non-native stoat – a larger cousin of the weasel. It is a fast-breeding carnivore which eats 25% of its body weight daily. With no natural predators to keep its numbers in check, stoats pose a major threat to Orkney's native wildlife, including the unique Orkney vole: see page 28.

The invasive stoat

To optimise your wildlife sightings, try to go out in early mornings or late evenings, carry binoculars, and move quietly.

The Way includes extensive road-walking in some sections: enjoy the wildflowers and butterflies in Orkney's verges. The Council plans its verge maintenance to promote biodiversity as well as road safety. From May to July, bright purple Northern marsh orchids flower all over the place: see below.

Northern marsh orchid

Coastal

Risso's dolphin

Much of the Way runs along the Mainland's coastal margin, in places along beaches, elsewhere along clifftops. The underlying rock has weathered to form cliffs with ledges that suit breeding seabirds, and the confluence of Atlantic waters with the North Sea makes Orkney's seas rich in plankton, and therefore fish and cetaceans.

This is one of the best places in the UK to see whales and dolphins, with records of 12 species ranging from harbour porpoise to humpback and sperm whales which visit Scapa Flow. There are also visits from orca pods, and up to five species of dolphin – of which Risso's is the most common in Orkney waters. To maximise your chances of a sighting, choose a time when the sea state is calm, pick a good vantage point and be prepared to wait: patience and luck are both vital.

Seals are much easier to spot, and you may even notice them swimming along beside you as you walk along the shore. The two kinds of seal you may see are common (harbour) seals and Atlantic greys – of which Orkney alone has about 15% of the world's population. Grey seals have distinctive heads with a Roman nose, whereas common seals have more dog-like heads with a rounded forehead and V-shaped nostrils. They often arch their sleek bodies when ashore, whereas greys look more lumpish when resting. They breed at different times, with pups born during June-July to common seals and October-November to grey seals.

Grey seal

Time spent resting ashore and basking on rocks is important to the health of seals of both kinds. It's better to use binocular than to approach closely: the criterion is that if your presence affects their behaviour, let alone causes them to move off, you are too close and should back off.

Orkney's plankton-rich waters support a wide range of fish in plenty, which in turn support a wide range of seabird life. Breeding seabirds congregate to breed here, with nearly a million seabirds scattered over the islands.

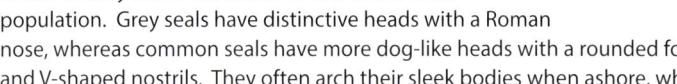

Eider duck (male)

Commonly seen are guillemots, kittiwakes and razorbills, with the stiff-winged fulmar (a small cousin of the albatross) also widespread.

The cliffs are also home to pigeons and rock doves, favourite prey of the peregrine falcon. The fastest bird in the world, it attains speeds of over 180 mph (290 kph) when it dives to catch birds on the wing.

Those seeking to view puffins will need to time their visit carefully. Puffins spend most of their lives at sea, fishing for sand eels, and returning to land only to breed in burrows. Their breeding season runs from April/May until late July/early August. Most of Orkney's puffins breed on the very remote lighthouse island of Sule Skerry, 40 miles west of the Mainland. However, they can also be seen on the Brough of Birsay, especially on its west side: time your visit well and stay vigilant about the tide: see page 39.

Peregrine falcon

Orkney is also home to the tiny Scottish primrose. It grows on Scotland's north coast (Caithness and Sutherland) and on certain of Orkney's islands, but nowhere else in the world. Although present on the Mainland (e.g. at Yesnaby), it is more prevalent on Rousay, Westray and Hoy. A good place to find it is the Hill of White Hamars, the nature reserve on South Walls, Hoy.

Back in the 1980s, two farmers found that selective grazing could benefit scarce plants, and within a decade had achieved a 500% increase in the Scottish primrose numbers. Generally similar to a miniature primrose, its tiny purple petals have yellow centres. Its first flowering period is late May, and the second, usually more productive, in July or even August.

Puffin

Scottish primrose (Primula scotica)

Moorland

Short-eared owl

The higher parts of Mainland are covered in heather moorland, a habitat that the Way traverses between Finstown and Orphir, and also east of Waulkmill Bay (Hobbister Hill). The moorland is rich in invertebrates, and it provides food and shelter for the endemic Orkney vole. This is a subspecies of the common field vole but it grows larger, with shorter, paler fur and bald ears.

Orkney voles run fast and are good swimmers, and they are present on seven of Orkney's islands in addition to its Mainland. On land, they often stand, meerkat-like, to scan their surroundings. Active in the daytime, they may take cover in burrows or shelter near ruined buildings, being favourite food of birds of prey.

Since their arrival in 2010, stoats have been preying upon voles, and also endangering rare populations of ground-nesting birds by eating their eggs and chicks. This includes rare species such as curlews, lapwings, oystercatchers and corncrakes. The Orkney Native Wildlife Project is attempting the world's largest stoat eradication project, and you may notice their rectangular timber stoat traps beside the Way. See ***www.orkneynativewildlife.org.uk*** for more information or to report a stoat sighting. Your help is appreciated.

Other moorland creature include brown hares, which feed on young grass shoots, and birds including meadow pipits, skylarks, snipe and golden plover. Soaring above, look for birds of prey, notably kestrels, short-eared owls and even hen harriers. The latter is the UK's rarest bird of prey, and Orkney hosts 20% of the UK's breeding population. All of these prey on the Orkney vole, so the stoat is threatening these lovely birds by competing fiercely for their food supply.

Orkney vole

Marshes and lochs

Red-throated diver

Recent years have seen a marked decline in marshland, and in the size of smaller lochs, as a result of 'improved' drainage, mainly on agricultural land. This poses a problem for wading birds and waterfowl. The lochs form a vital winter haven for tens of thousands of migrating waterfowl, some of which rest for a while before continuing south, whilst others choose to stay over winter.

The smaller lochs are home to mallard, teal, red-breasted merganser and the rare red-throated diver. The larger lochs that the Way passes (Swannay, Boardhouse and Harray) are important breeding sites for waders of all kinds, and for swans, geese and ducks.

The greylag is the UK's largest wild goose, and large numbers from Iceland visit Orkney and overwinter there. Back in the 1980s they were autumn migrants, heading south in winter and only a few hundred stayed on in Orkney. Nowadays, warmer winters mean that the geese have no incentive to move on, so they graze in Orkney all winter. Large numbers create serious damage to crops and NatureScot is working with the Orkney Goose Management Group to try to reduce the population to 5000 birds.

There are at least 11 species of duck of which mallard, teal, tufted and wigeon are most common. The rare pintail is found on west Mainland, but you would be lucky to see one. The resident swans are mainly the familiar mute variety, but noisy whooper swans arrive from Iceland in autumn – some on their way further south, others (like greylag geese) finding Orkney so much to their taste that they overwinter here.

Pintail duck

3.1 Egilsay

Distance	3·4 miles 5·4 km
Terrain	a short, easy walk, mainly on road with a mile of track and some beach walking
Grade	fairly flat
Food and drink	community centre (hot drink making facilities)
Summary	a half-day excursion to a scenic small island to visit historic sites associated with St Magnus

```
0·0        1·4           beach            2·0           3·4
ferry      2·2                             3·2          ferry
```

The ferry to Egilsay departs from Tingwall on the Mainland, 12 miles west and north of Kirkwall. Check the Orkney Ferries timetable carefully: see page 71. Your early afternoon return from Egilsay must be booked in advance through the website because the ferry stops at Egilsay only on request. Half a day gives you plenty of time to explore the island.

- On arrival, follow the road up to the waiting-room which has a toilet and information about the RSPB Onziebust nature reserve which covers over half the island. Follow the road as it winds gently uphill past Midskaill Farm on the right with the distinctive round tower of St Magnus Church visible across the fields on the left.

- As you approach the top of the hill, stay on the road – ignoring the wooden sign indicating St Magnus Church for now – and within 600 m reach a crossroads. Go straight across, along the unmetalled road. Immediately on the left is the Egilsay community centre in the old schoolhouse with a toilet, sitting room and kitchen for making drinks. There is wifi and an honesty box.

St Magnus Church, Egilsay

- Afterwards continue east on the rough road through an open gate with a notice welcoming you to RSPB Onziebust. There's a good view of the island of Eday ahead.
- Just 120 m from the crossroads, go through a waymarked kissing-gate on the right into a field. Walk along the western edge of the field, through another kissing-gate and on to the St Magnus Memorial in the next field – one of the traditional sites of St Magnus' death: see page 21.
- Retrace your steps back through the two gates to the rough road and turn right to continue east. After 300 m the road reaches a waymarked gate. On its far side cattle may be grazing and the road becomes a rougher track.
- Follow the track through another gate, still heading east. After the track ends, continue to and through a gate. Reach the beautiful sandy beach at Nettle Knowe and the South Geo of Canquoy, where Magnus and Håkon's ships may have landed.
- After exploring the shore, retrace your steps to the crossroads by the community centre. Here turn right, heading north. Within 300 m of the crossroads, turn left as signed to St Magnus Church and its graveyard: see the panel on page 31.
- Afterwards retrace your steps to the crossroads. Here a right turn will take you straight back to the ferry pier.
- If you have time in hand, instead continue ahead (south), uphill through the RSPB reserve. Within 500 m reach a spectacular viewpoint over many islands in the archipelago, with an information board. With binoculars, you can even see Kirkwall and the spire of St Magnus Cathedral. Be sure to return to the pier in good time for the ferry.

St Magnus Memorial

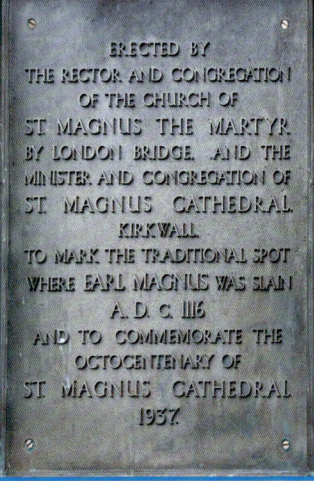

Sandy beach at Nettle Knowe

3.2 Gurness to Birsay

| | | 35 | 36 | 37 | 40 |

Distance 13·4 miles 21·6 km
Terrain some challenging and varied terrain, from broken coastal ground and pathless hillside to 3 miles of quiet road-walking
Grade only one notable height gain, to 152 m on Costa Hill, but many small undulations
Food and drink Evie (1·6 miles offroute), Birsay (café and shop), Swannay Brewery (café, 800 m offroute)
Summary varied walking from a fortified village to St Magnus Church via glorious coastal scenery with fine views

0·0 — 2·7 Grugar / A966 — 4·0 — Costa Hill — 2·9 — Ramly Geo — 3·8 — 13·4
Gurness   4·3   6·5   4·7   6·1   Birsay

- Begin at the Broch of Gurness, which may be where Magnus' body was brought ashore. Take the chance to visit Scotland's best-preserved fortified village, dating from the Iron Age. (If you arrive out of hours, you may not be able to buy a ticket, but very likely can still explore the site.)
- Follow the visitor route, which approaches the broch's impressive entrance in an anticlockwise loop, and learn more from the excellent interpretation boards.

Broch of Gurness
This is one of the best-preserved examples of a broch – a unique Iron Age circular stone structure – in all Scotland. The Broch of Gurness is on a grand scale, and may originally have stood 12-13 metres tall – four times the height of the remains that you see today. Brochs have a single entrance and no windows, so they were easy to defend.
An archaeologist has estimated that its construction required 3226 person-days – equivalent to nine people working full-time for a year. Inside the broch there's a network of chambers, and clustered around it are houses and workshops that suggest how its Iron Age inhabitants lived.

Broch of Gurness

Stepping stones across the Burn of Desso

- After the broch, return to the car park and notice the carved waystone: see page 35. Look for a themed waystone at the start of each section of the Way.
- Walk back along the road, which soon runs above the Sands of Evie. From the road above, you'll be able to assess whether you can cross the burn (and therefore walk along the beach).
- If the beach looks viable, within 400 m of the car park descend sharp right on a path of sorts, head for the stepping stones and take whatever route along the beach seems best. Skip the next bullet.
- Around high tide, however, the burn will be awash. Stay on the road for a further 400 m to reach a T-junction: turn sharp right along the minor road across the burn and continue above the beach.
- At mile 1 you join the beach route across the sands at Aikerness. The car park here has public toilets, and a bothy which offers good shelter in foul weather.
- From Aikerness the Way continues along the coast on some of the roughest terrain in the entire route. If the tide is high or your agility limited, you may prefer to bypass the next 2·2 km by turning left up the road from the toilets. After 900 m, reach the A966, turn right and rejoin the route after a further 1·9 km at a beautiful carved bench. Skip to page 36, end of bullet 3.
- Otherwise take care over the next section, especially in the wet: if the tide is low there will be more scope to pick your route. At high tide you may be forced onto a challenging path over broken ground at the top of the beach, sometimes overgrown. Lower down is often easier, and at least the hazards of slippery rocks and seaweed are more obvious.

Beach walking at mid tide

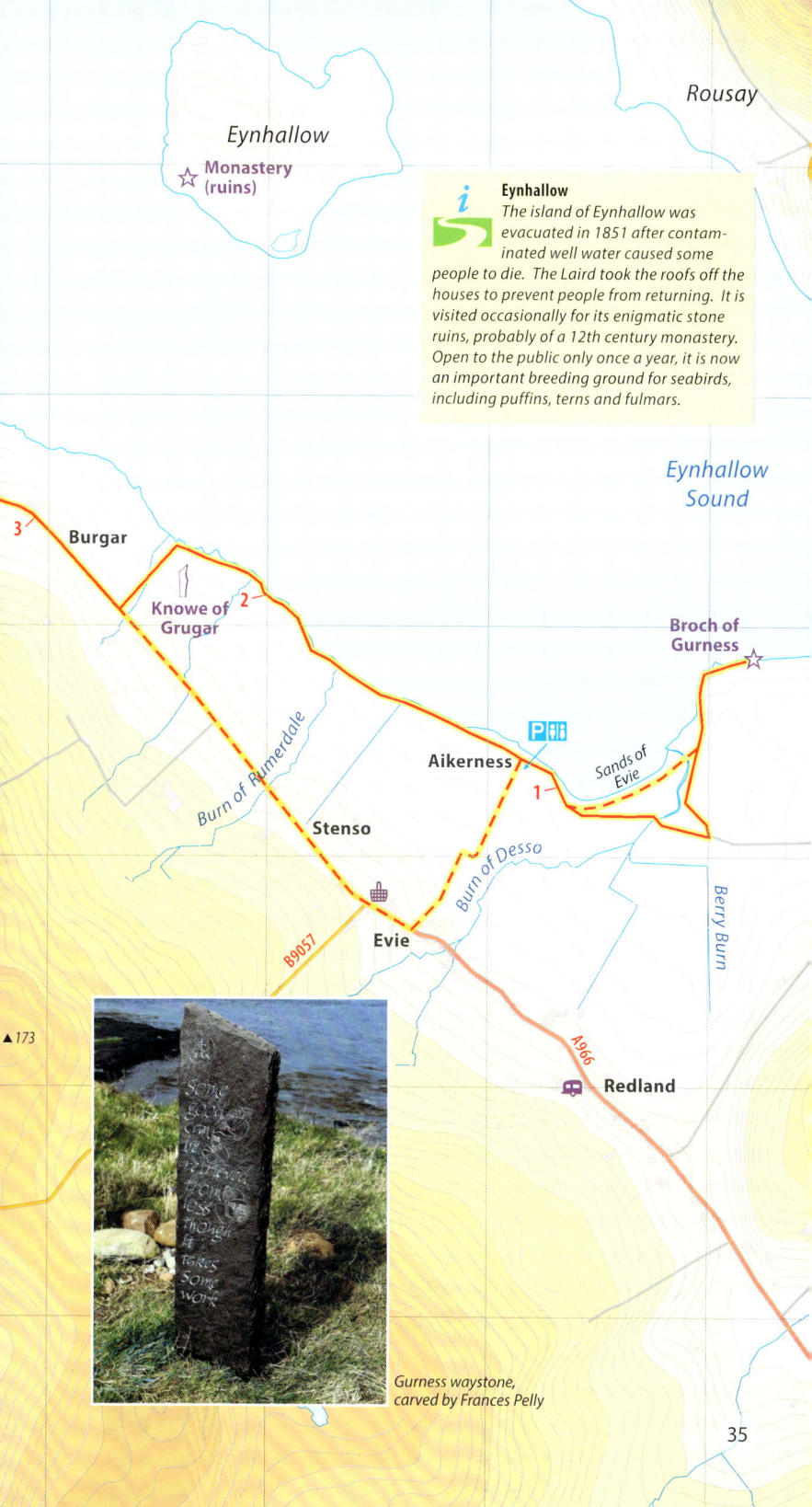

Eynhallow

The island of Eynhallow was evacuated in 1851 after contaminated well water caused some people to die. The Laird took the roofs off the houses to prevent people from returning. It is visited occasionally for its enigmatic stone ruins, probably of a 12th century monastery. Open to the public only once a year, it is now an important breeding ground for seabirds, including puffins, terns and fulmars.

Gurness waystone, carved by Frances Pelly

Eynhallow from the Way

- Whatever route you choose, be sure to pause from time to time so as to look around: there may be a seal basking on rocks, seabirds overhead or eider ducklings bobbing on the water.
- After about 2 km of slow going, you reach the remains of the Knowe of Grugar, a grassy mound about 30 m in diameter and 5 m high, believed to be full of stones and probably housing a broch and outbuildings.
- Just afterwards (mile 2·5), turn left up a waymarked grassy track between a stone wall and fence. Within 400 m it reaches the road at Grugar, where you turn right. The road affords a fine view to the right over Eynhallow Sound to Rousay. For more on Eynhallow, see the panel on page 35.

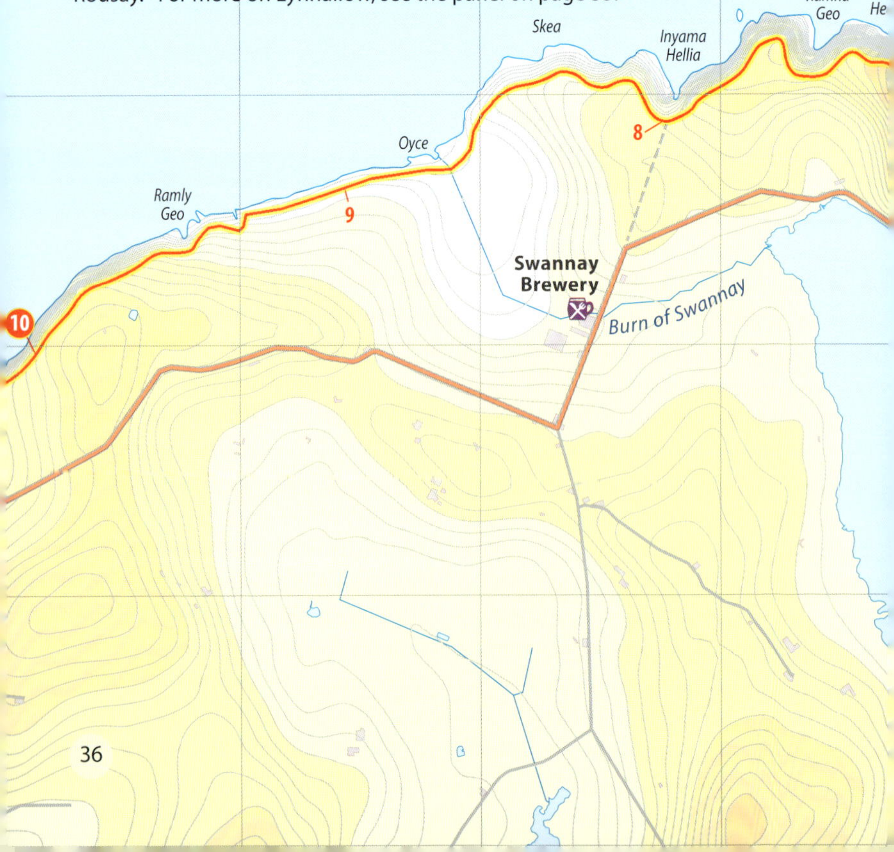

South-west over Loch of Swannay from Costa summit

- The Way now follows the A966 for about 3 miles (5 km), towards your next goal, Costa Hill, with improving views over the Loch of Swannay on your left. Near the far end of the loch, look for the entrance to a track that heads sharp right uphill (mile 6).
- Go through the kissing-gate onto a track which winds its way upwards, with plenty of bends to ease the gradient and increasingly fine views as you ascend. The summit is marked with a trig point and although its altitude is only 151 m, it provides an excellent viewpoint over the Mainland.

- Pass by a long low stone building, a survivor from military use in World War 2. It offers some shelter from high winds, and from there you will see waymarker posts ↘ taking you north-westerly down from the summit area. The hillside is mainly pathless, but the waymarker posts are normally intervisible – unless there is dense sea fog or low cloud.

Wartime building, Costa Hill

- The waymarkers lead you to a gate, and from here you embark on a section where the route is less clearly defined. In general, keep the sea on your right, never go too close to a cliff edge – especially in windy weather – and never cross a barbed wire fence. There are some waymarkers on gates and fence pillars, but little in between.
- Follow the fenceline around the first two geos, Ramna Geo and Inyama Hellia (mile 8). To detour to the Swannay Brewery with café, turn left up a track: first check its opening times: **www.swannaybrewery.com.**
- Continue along the coast passing through a gate and descending. At Oyce, cross the Burn of Swannay on a narrow bridge (mile 8·7).
- After a further 900 m reach Ramly Geo, where a gate protects the cliff edge. Continue along the coast, soon gaining your first sight of the Brough of Birsay offshore ahead.
- Still keeping back from the cliff edge, continue down past the Loop of Crooie to Whitaloo Point. Steep timber steps and handrails help you across two steep geos, then you climb out of a third dip on further steps.
- At mile 11, go through the kissing-gate towards two old military buildings, along the spectacular cliffs of Whitaloo Geo.
- Beyond the buildings, either use the stile across the fence to follow the narrow clifftop path, or else stay inside the field beside the fence and after 200 m rejoin the path via a kissing-gate. Continue westward along the top of the cliffs.

Whitaloo Geo

Whalebone near Skipi Geo

- At mile 11·8 the Way goes through another kissing-gate on the approach to Hesta Geo. A short descent from the path will afford a much better view of this formation.
- The photo above shows the clifftop site of the whalebone sculpture created from parts of the jawbone and skull of a right whale washed up in 1876 on the beach below. It may have marked the long connection between Orcadians and whales, and perhaps also served as a landmark for fishing boats.
- Continue to Skipi (Skibba) Geo with its restored fishing hut and well-preserved nousts (rounded hollows in the ground for storing boats).
- Continue to the car park at the Point of Buckquoy, with its causeway to the Brough of Birsay, a tidal island. Beside it are picnic tables with some shelter from the wind. Before deciding to cross the causeway, make sure you know the tide times: the causeway is safe for only about two hours either side of low tide. See page 70 for sources of tidal predictions.

The Brough of Birsay
This tidal island is full of interest: it features on our front cover and in the photo below. The ruins of the important Norse settlement and medieval monastery are open all year. The dramatic cliffs to the north and west of the island are home to many nesting birds, including breeding puffins between April and July. The lighthouse is at its north-west extreme and was built in 1925 by David Stevenson, member of the famous lighthouse family.

East over the ruins of the monastery and Norse village

- To enjoy the island fully, try to allow at least an hour. Cross the slippery stones and causeway with care, then climb the ramp beyond. Begin with a clockwise tour of the island's coastal cliffs and lighthouse, then enjoy the Norse village and monastery remains once you can keep an eye on the causeway.
- Once safely back at the car park, follow the road towards Birsay village. At mile 13·4 the road bends left just before you turn right at the Earl's Palace. Earl Robert Stewart began building the palace in 1574 and its ruins are well worth exploring. Enter through the kissing-gate: the palace is always open.
- Just beyond, the section officially ends at St Magnus Church, with its fine stained-glass window: see page 21. Next door there's a shop (Palace Stores) and – although the Way soon leaves this road – you may want to detour to visit the tearoom 350 m further south. For opening times, see *www.birsaybaytearoom.co.uk* (tel 01856 721 399).

3·3 Birsay to Dounby

Distance	10·4 miles 16·7 km
Terrain	about 60% on quiet roads, with the rest offroad on tracks
Grade	mostly gentle gradients with no steep sections except on optional climb up Greeny Hill
Food and drink	Birsay (shop) and Dounby (shop, hotel)
Summary	undemanding walking with many points of interest – from a working mill to standing stones and, if conditions suit a hill climb, superb views from Greeny Hill

```
13·4      2·8    Wheebin     4·5      Midhouse Farm    3·1       23·8
○─────────────────○─────────────────○─────────────────○─────────○
Birsay    4·5                7·2                       5·0     Dounby
```

- From St Magnus Church follow the road south past the Palace Stores. Cross the Burn of Boardhouse by the bridge (public toilets on its far side) and turn left immediately. The Way is about to follow a detour east to the Barony Mill and Mans Well (1·2 miles round trip) by a grassy track that runs beside the burn.

- Within 80 m the road becomes a grassy track at a metal farm gate: check whether a notice advises you against this route. If so, your options are either to omit this detour altogether, or, if keen to visit the Barony Mill, backtrack to turn east along the A966, then right down the A967. Afterwards retrace your steps to the bridge in Birsay, making a 2·8-mile round trip. Skip to bullet 2 on page 42.

- If there is no warning against proceeding, go through the gate and follow the overgrown track beside the burn. This section may be very muddy and perhaps waterlogged in places.

- The track becomes firmer underfoot and reaches the road (A967 with bus stop) in front of the Barony Mill – the last remaining working mill in Orkney. In season, it is open for visits and 30-minute guided tours: see its website *www.baronymill.com*.

- Turn left on the road across the burn, and within 50 m turn right onto the minor road for Kirbuster. The ancient Mans Well, said never to run dry, is just 80 m beyond on the right: see photo above.

South-east over the Earl's Palace and St Magnus Church, Birsay

- Different traditions claim that Magnus used the well himself, that his body was rested here on its way to Birsay or that his remains were washed here, all linking its pure waters with healing. Its water is also used in brewing beer and is added to whisky, especially at new year.
- From the well, retrace your steps back to the bridge in Birsay and turn left (south).
- Within 20 m turn right off the road onto a grassy path towards the beach. (For the Birsay Bay tearoom stay on the road for 300 m but check its opening times: see page 40.)

- After 50 m of grassy path go through a kissing-gate onto the links where there may be cattle, but they are used to walkers. The path narrows and soon reaches the low cliffs above the beach.
- Turn left, passing through a blue wooden gate and follow the path along the top of the cliffs, enjoying fine coastal walking with views north to the Brough of Birsay and south to Marwick Head.
- After the low cliffs give way to sand dunes, you may like to explore the beach. Birsay Bay is a good spot for bird watching, and grey seals often haul out on the rocks and beach.
- The path becomes sandy and less distinct as it continues on the seaward side of a large dune. Before the end of the bay it turns left inland and joins a wider track at mile 15·1.
- Follow the track through a metal gate and onto a tarmac road uphill. After 400 m of tarmac, turn left onto the minor road which after 850 m passes the Orkney Antique Centre on the right. The views include the Brough of Birsay to your left and the Loch of Boardhouse ahead.
- Just before the T-junction with the A967 notice the impressive Wheebin stone standing four metres tall in the field on the right. The folklore belief is that on every new year's day, the stone strolls down to the nearby loch for a drink.
- Turn right to follow the A967 for the next 3 km, following advice on road-walking at the foot of page 13. The road runs parallel to the loch shore, for 1·7 km where it bends.

The Wheebin stone

- Look in a field on the left for the Strathyre stone, although it may be partly obscured by crops in the field. This is the only Mans Stone still standing. Such stones were used to rest the body of Magnus on its long journey: see page 21.

- Continue uphill on the A967 heading south. After 800 m pass a group of houses and the former Twatt Church (built in 1874, and now privately owned). From Twatt, descend to the junction where the A967 turns off right for Stromness but the Way keeps ahead, briefly on the A986.

Strathyre Mans Stone

- After a further 300 m, turn left onto the quiet Hundland road signed for Kirbuster, Hundland and Swannay. Follow it for nearly 1 km, with Costa Hill visible ahead to the left.

- At mile 18·6 the road bends left for the Kirbuster Farm Museum, but the Way turns off right. To visit the excellent museum would take only an 800-m detour from here, but check the opening times on its website: ***bit.ly/SMW-kirbuster***.

- Otherwise, the Way bears right uphill on the very minor Durkadale road. Follow it for 1·3 km towards the Loch of Hundland. The RSPB Birsay Moors reserve is nearby, an important site for hen harriers, red-throated divers and arctic skuas.

- At a sign for Canada Farm (mile 19·5) turn right off the road onto a waymarked track. After a few metres, at another fork bear right and continue uphill on the gravel farm track.

- Leave the track where it curves right towards the house, and continue uphill on a waymarked grassy path to the left of a fence, heading towards a wind turbine.

- At the turbine, make a right-left dogleg and continue between fields along the western shoulder of Greeny Hill. The views here are expansive, with the Brough of Birsay and the sea visible to the right and the hills of Hoy ahead.

 The path, overgrown in places, briefly merges with a track heading in the same direction before meeting a rope barrier: step over or loosen it to pass through. Continue in the same direction along an overgrown section of broken ground with drainage channels: take care where you place your boots.

Descending to Greeny

North-west from the summit of Greeny Hill

- Once you join the farm track, difficulties are over and at Midhouse Farm (mile 20·7), you join a minor road leading downhill. Loch of Harray is visible ahead to the left, beyond Dounby village, with a distant glimpse of Scapa Flow. On a clear day you may see the highest point on the Mainland ahead to the right – a ridge with Mid Hill and Ward Hill (275 m and 268 m) and the hills of Hoy distant beyond.
- Descend on the road to the T-junction at Greeny. Turn left and continue on the minor road which becomes a gravel track at the farm Nether Fea (mile 21·3).
- Bear left uphill on the track past a sign for Shady Neuk. The track levels and passes this house before climbing again on a waymarked grassy path through gorse. At the top, join a minor road and follow it uphill.
- After 400 m reach Cloke Farm, with a sign for the walkway to Greeny Hill summit (2·1 km round trip). This detour takes under an hour and on a clear day is highly recommended: the views are stunning, with Hoy and Scapa Flow to the south, and Costa Hill, Rousay and distant Westray visible to the north.
- The Way continues along the road from the farm, passing scattered buildings. Follow it around to the right and descend towards Dounby.
- The road crosses the Burn of Beaquoy and climbs slightly for 600 m to meet the B9057 at a T-junction. To reach Dounby's facilities, turn right here for 800 m.
- Within 40 m of this right turn, note the waymarker pointing left up the road to North Bigging. For nearly all walkers, this belongs to the next section of the Way. However, walkers in a serious hurry may want to bypass Dounby and follow this sign: see page 9.
- The Way into Dounby passes public toilets on the right, and ends at the Market Green at Dounby crossroads. The bus stop is to the right, just beyond the Smithfield Hotel.

From Greeny Hill, south-south-west to Hoy

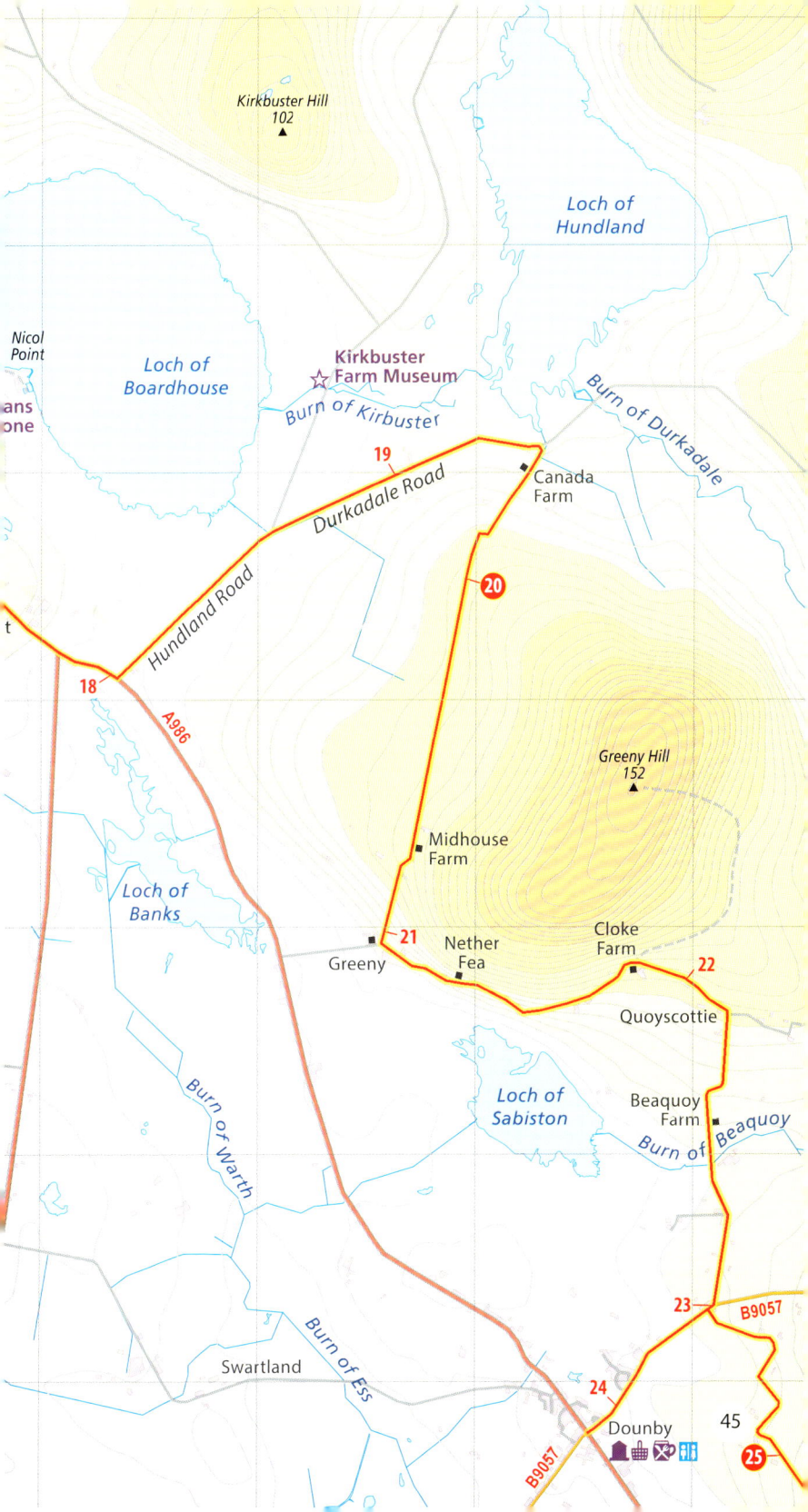

3.4 Dounby to Finstown

Distance 10·3 miles 16·6 km
Terrain largely road walking (74%), mainly on very minor roads, the rest is on paths and tracks through field and woodland
Grade generally flat with some gentle gradients and very little ascent overall
Food and drink Dounby, Merkister Hotel, Finstown
Summary varied inland walking, from lochside to rare woodland via an isolated church and graveyard, ending at the coast

23·8		3·6	Loch of Harray		4·0		A986	2·7		34·1
Dounby		5·8			6·4				4·3	Finstown

- From the Dounby crossroads, retrace your steps at the end of 3.3 for 800 m. Take the B9057 north-east out of the village, using its pavement at first, then cross over to face oncoming traffic. Turn off right on the road to North Bigging, just 40 m short of the road from Beaquoy that you used yesterday.
- Follow the road around its twists and turns, the height affording views across the Loch of Harray to the hills of Hoy. After 1·8 km it reaches its high point near Holodyke House.
- At mile 25·5 the road turns sharp right, heads downhill past the farm of North Bigging and winds down to reach the A986 within 1·1 km.

Drovers' track

- Cross straight over the main road and continue ahead past the stables to Howaback. At mile 26·7 you meet an old drovers' track: turn left to follow this ancient route for 800 m to its end. Conyar is an indistinct mound on the left.
- Turn right at Russland Road, which soon reaches the Merkister Hotel. Follow the road around to the left and along the shore of the Loch of Harray. Pass Mill Cottage, a refurbished former water mill.

Across Loch of Harray to the Merkister Hotel

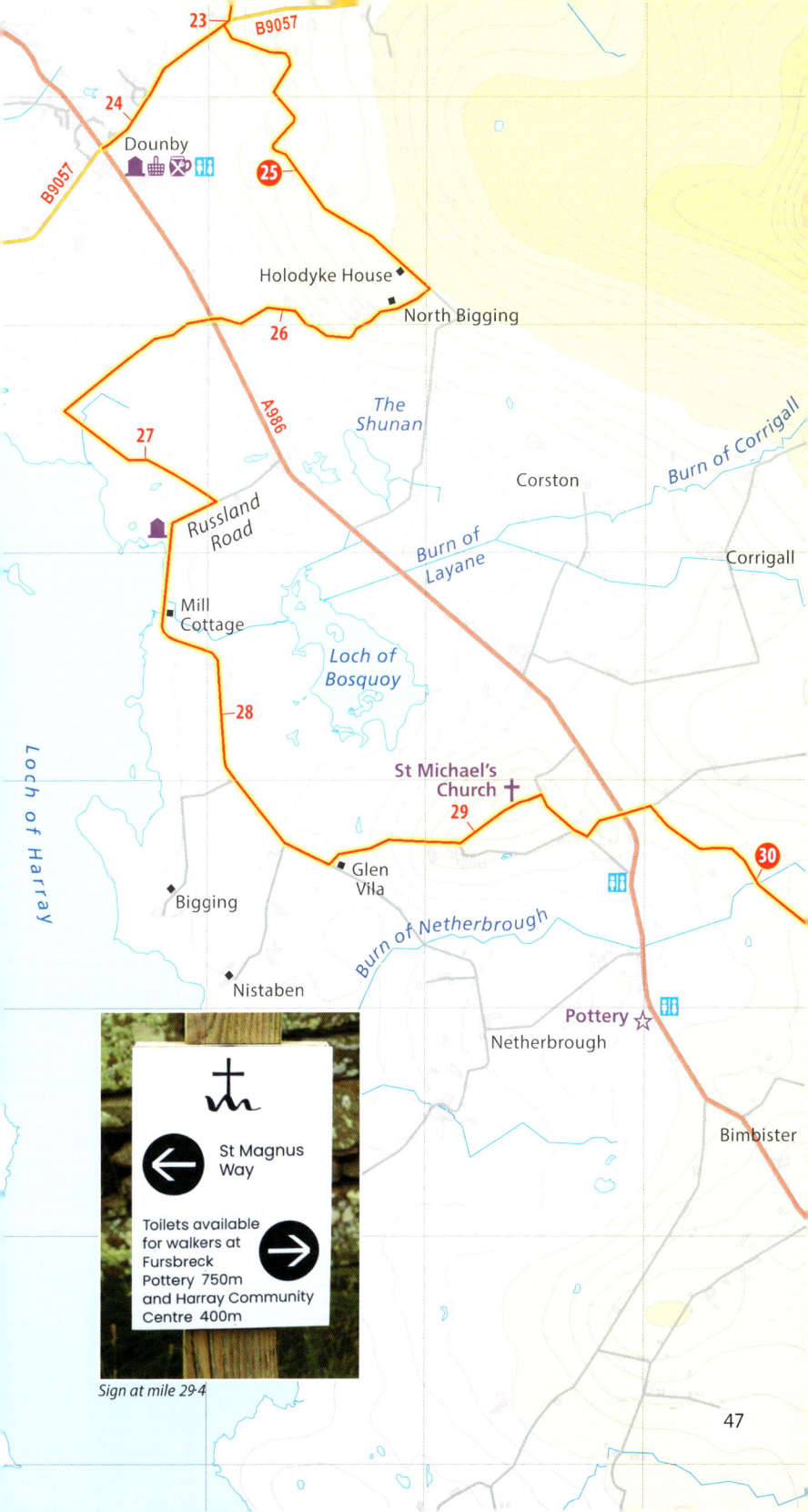

Across the graveyard to St Michael's Church

- The road then leaves the lochside and continues inland. Ignore roads to the right (signed for Bigging and Nistaben), but just after the latter, at mile 28·6 (Glen Villa) a waymarker points you left onto a farm track uphill to Quean.
- Continue up the track past some farm buildings, then take the grassy path to the left that leads to St Michael's Church. This stands on a spectacular site, but sadly it is generally kept locked except for services.
- However, there is plenty of interest in the graveyard. Visit its war memorial, located on top of a small broch (grassy mound) which provides a panorama of Harray in every direction. Among many interesting graves, those of the author Eric Linklater (1899-1974) and his wife Marjorie (1909-97) rest side by side at the wall: see below.
- After you exit the graveyard entrance, turn left and follow the road down to the junction (100 m). Turn right downhill for 300 m, then take the next left uphill to reach the A986 – unless following the sign for a toilet detour (mile 29·4).

The graves of Marjorie and Eric Linklater

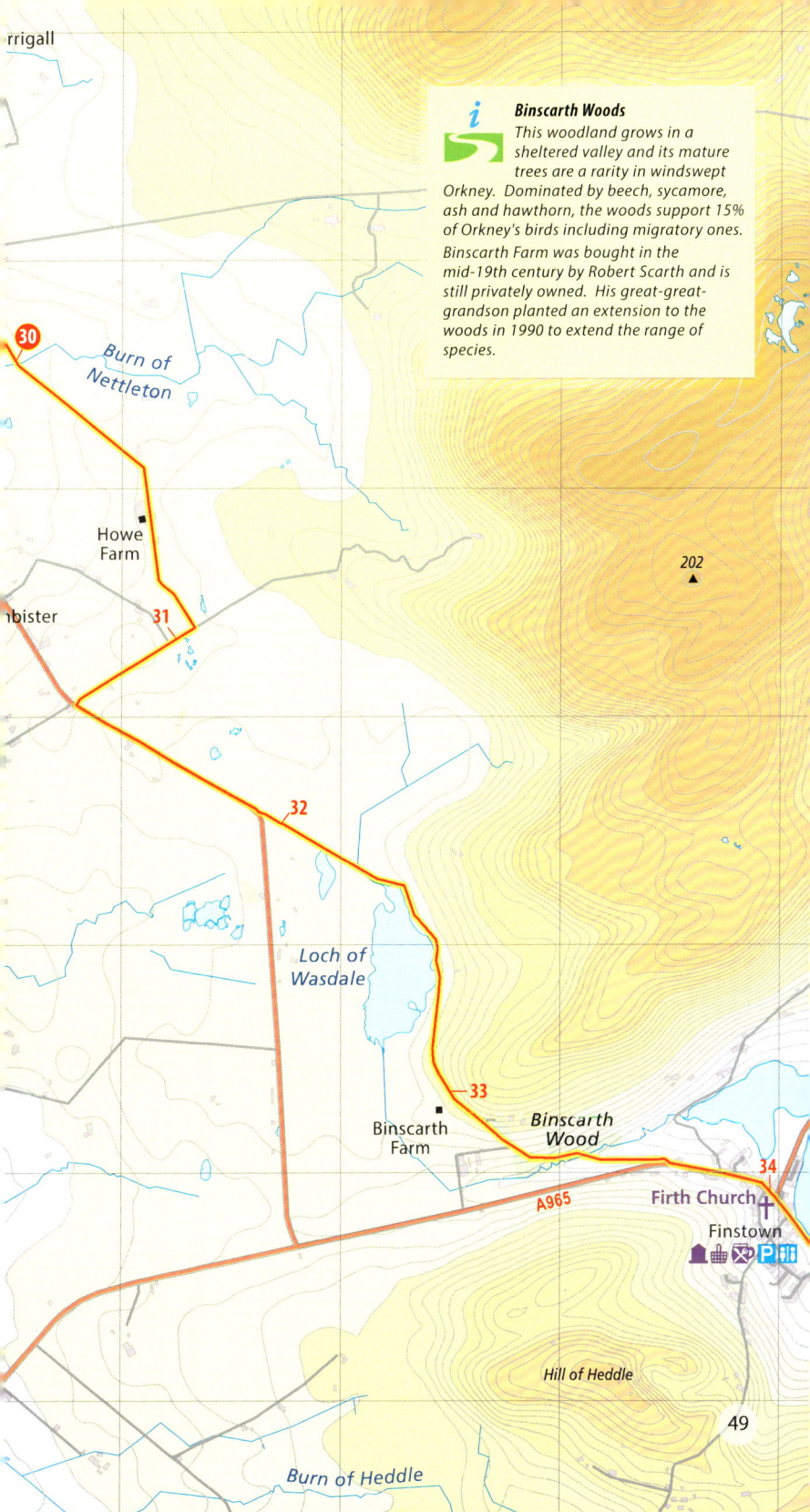

Loch of Wasdale

- Cross straight over onto Lyde Road and after 140 m turn right, signed for Howe. This quiet single-track road soon crosses the Burn of Nettleton and bears right past Howe Farm.
- At the T-junction (mile 30·9), turn right opposite a small car park and continue on the minor road for just over 600 m to the A986.
- Turn left along the busy Harray Road. After 1 km, the road turns sharp right at Refuge Corner, but the Way goes straight ahead on a broad, loose-surfaced track (mile 31·9).
- Follow the track beside the Loch of Wasdale, keeping watch for teal, wigeon and mute swans on its waters. Head uphill through a gate and continue on the grassy path as it climbs and joins the Binscarth Farm road, where you bear right.

Finstown and Wideford Hill across the bay

Binscarth Woods

- Where the road bends right, leave it to go through the waymarked gate onto a track through Binscarth Woods directly ahead: see the panel on page 49.
- The woods can be muddy: the direct route continues straight down the track, but if you go through any of the gates off to the right you may enjoy a beautiful if muddy woodland walk beside a burn before returning to the main track.
- At the bottom of the hill the track crosses the burn and leads out of the woods through a kissing-gate. There are sometimes cattle in the next field, which leads you up a grassy slope to another kissing-gate (mile 33·7).
- Exit onto the main road for the final 900 m into Finstown, crossing the road with care, and turning left downhill past Baikie's Stores. Keep on the pavement down the right hand side of the road past Firth Church.
- Then cross the road to the pavement along the shore side to reach the car park at Finstown overlooking the Bay of Firth. The section ends at the interpretation board and waystone.

North-west over the Bay of Firth (right), Finstown to the lower left

3.5 Finstown to Orphir

Distance	9.6 miles 15.4 km
Terrain	road walking is 45%, the rest is on tracks and rough paths
Grade	starts with climb to 160 m on Lyradale Hill, undulating thereafter
Food and drink	none outside Finstown: carry or arrange supplies
Summary	charming section that crosses from east coast to south, with fine views and a splendid finale at Orphir Round Church

```
34.1        2.4    Hill of Lyradale      4.1         A964        3.1    43.7
○───────────────────────▲────────────────────○──────────────○───────────○
Finstown    3.9                             6.6                  5.0    Orphir
```

- Start from the car park by the shore, with Leigh's famous food van – which when open offers 'a real taste of Orkney'. Leave the toilets on your left and follow the road to Esson's garage, where you cross over.

- Bear right up the Old Finstown Road, and after 120 m turn right up a road past the Firth Community Centre. Continue uphill past houses and Rowan Cottage (self-catering). The road soon morphs into a waymarked grassy track leading uphill across heather moorland.

- Within 300 m of the last house, a waymarker turns you left up a narrow path towards some scattered stone cairns and pillars, created playfully some 25 years ago by local people. As you climb, look behind you for fine views over Finstown and the Bay of Firth.

- As you crest the hill, locate the waymarker that is about to turn you right between two pillars. To visit Cuween Chambered Cairn (only 60 m offroute) instead turn left down a narrow path. Climb the tall stile at its entrance, where you will find information boards and a torch to borrow.

Cuween Chambered Cairn

Cuween is Old Norse for 'cattle pasture' and this tomb is still surrounded by grazing. It dates from 3100 BC and was excavated in 1901. In addition to human remains (mainly skulls) they found 24 dog skulls, dating from about 2600 BC.

The cairn's peaceful hilltop location makes for an atmospheric visit, though you need to crawl several metres through its low passageway to reach the main chamber. Once inside, there is room to stand, but the entrances to the four side chambers are very small.

Inside the cairn it's pitch dark: if you borrow the torch from the box outside, be sure to switch off when you return it.

Over the Bay of Firth from Cuween Hill

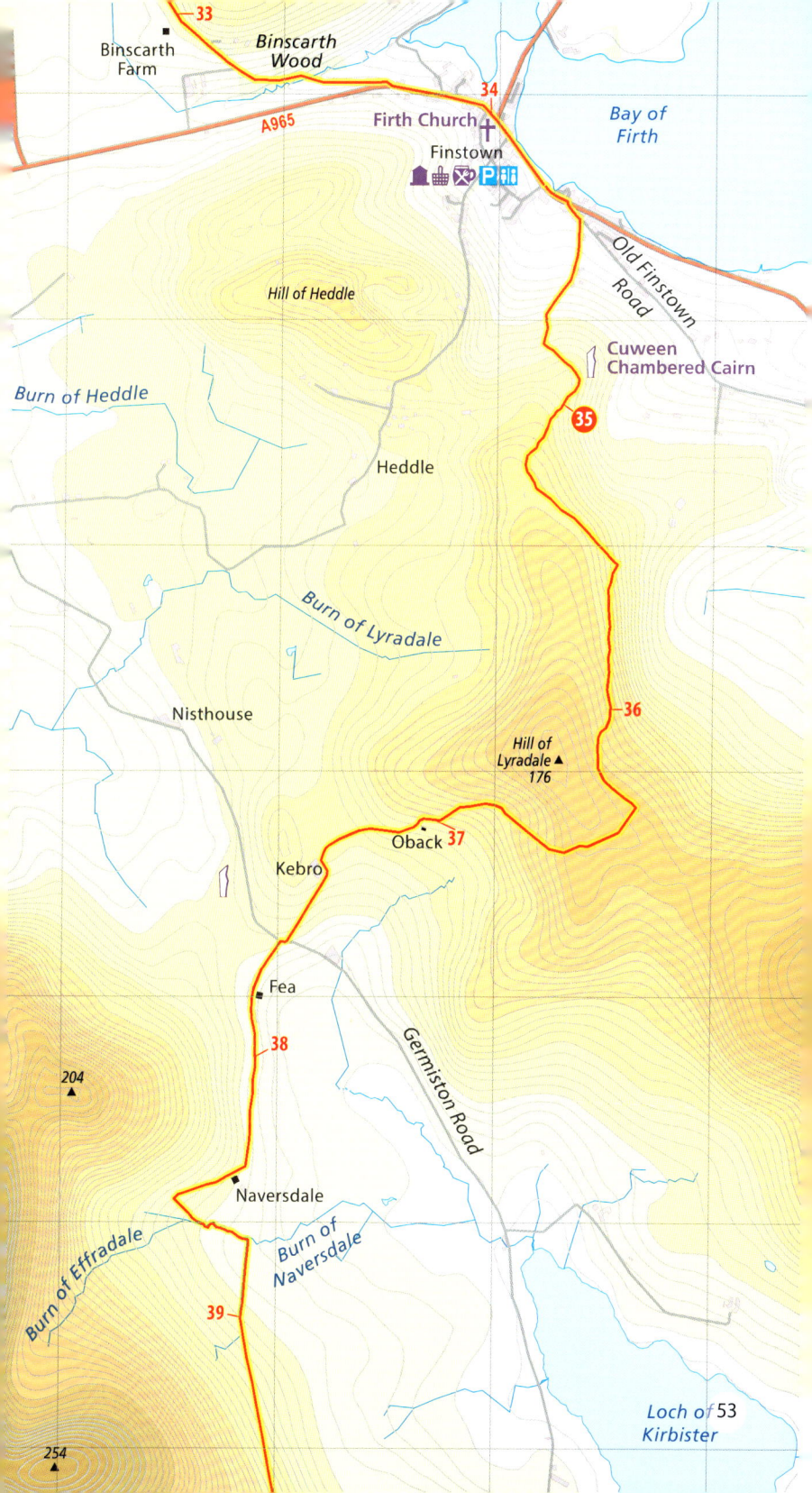

North over the Bay of Firth from Cuween Hill

- Afterwards continue uphill on the rough but well-defined path, following waymarkers to turn uphill at first, then contouring the hill. Keep looking behind you for fine views over the Bay of Firth and its islands.

- Continue ahead following waymarker posts across the moor. The path ends with a short descent to meet the Keelylang track, a broad gravel road, where you turn right (mile 35·6).

- Follow the track for 1·2 km uphill until it bends around to the left and flattens out, passing peat banks on the right (mile 36·3). Look for the waymarker on your right that turns you right up a path leading to a gate. (If you reach a cattle grid on the track before you turn off, you have overshot and should backtrack.)

Path leading to a gate

- At the far end of the peat bank go through the gate and enjoy splendid views from the Hill of Lyradale (176 m): the photo below looks south-east over Scapa Flow. On a clear day distant mountains appear to the south-south-west: these are in Sutherland, including Scotland's most northerly Munro, Ben Hope (927 m/3041 ft).

- Turn left to follow the rough path as it swings first right, then left, and descends past the buildings of Oback on a better surface. After 400 m it approaches the farm buildings at Kebro, but then bends left around them to descend to the Germiston Road (mile 37·7).
- At the road, make a right-left dogleg onto the road signed for Fea. After passing the farm, it's nearly 800 m to the house at Naversdale. This is where the Naversdale Stone was found in 2013. The runes on the stone transliterate into a fragment of the Lord's Prayer – rare evidence of Christian practice in a house during the medieval period.
- Just before the house, take the waymarked grassy track to its right. Follow this for 350 m to a ruined cottage where you turn left downhill beside a drainage ditch and fence.
- After a gate, turn left beside the Burn of Naversdale to reach a small timber footbridge (mile 38·7). Cross over and continue downstream on its far side on a trod path that is faint in places.

Footbridge across the Burn of Naversdale

- Pass through a pair of gates, then a third gate at an angle. This leads to the waymarked Burgir track where you turn right to head almost due south,
- Follow the track for the next 2·8 km, climbing at first, then levelling out with the track now broader and better drained. Continue as it descends past a reservoir down to reach the main road opposite the track to Swanbister.
- Turn right at the A964, walking on the right to face oncoming traffic until you reach pavement at the 'Welcome to Orphir village' sign, soon passing the school on the right. To reach the village B&Bs, keep ahead. Note that as of 2022 there were no cafés or food shops in Orphir.
- The Way continues by turning left down Gyre Road at Orphir Kirk, after 1·2 km beside the A964. Pass the Noust sign (claiming bar, restaurant and post Office) which as of 2022 was closed long term.

South-east over the mouth of Scapa Flow

The Bu Burn, Orphir

- Follow the road for 1·3 km to a large patch of trees. Bear left as signed for the Breck – a car park – which you reach within 1 km, just after the road bends left.
- Beyond the Breck interpretation board, follow the narrow path to the shore and turn right, heading north-west. After 1·2 km of coastline, the path crosses the Bu Burn on a footbridge and approaches Orphir graveyard.
- Turn right briefly and enter the graveyard through its side gate: the Round Kirk is diagonally ahead. Afterwards exit via the metal gates for the Earl's Bu (drinking hall) excavation and interpretation board. These foundations were discovered in 1859. According to the Saga, heavy drinking in the Bu led to violence and deaths – punctuated by brief visits to the kirk to atone.

> **Orphir Round Church**
> Scotland's only surviving circular church was built in the late 11th or early 12th century, probably by Earl Håkon. Its structure reflects that of the Church of the Holy Sepulchre in Jerusalem, where Håkon went on pilgrimage after the murder of his cousin Magnus. Dedicated to Saint Nicholas, the church was almost intact until the mid-18th century when parts were pulled down. The stones were used to build a long-gone parish church, and its graveyard still surrounds the Round Church.

- Visit the Orkneyinga Saga Centre ahead, open 9.00-18.00 daily from April to October. Its exhibition is free and it has public toilets. The audiovisual display draws imaginatively on the Saga and brings to life the story of the Norse earls. The Saga mentions both Round Church and Earl's Bu in its chapter 66.

Orphir Round Church

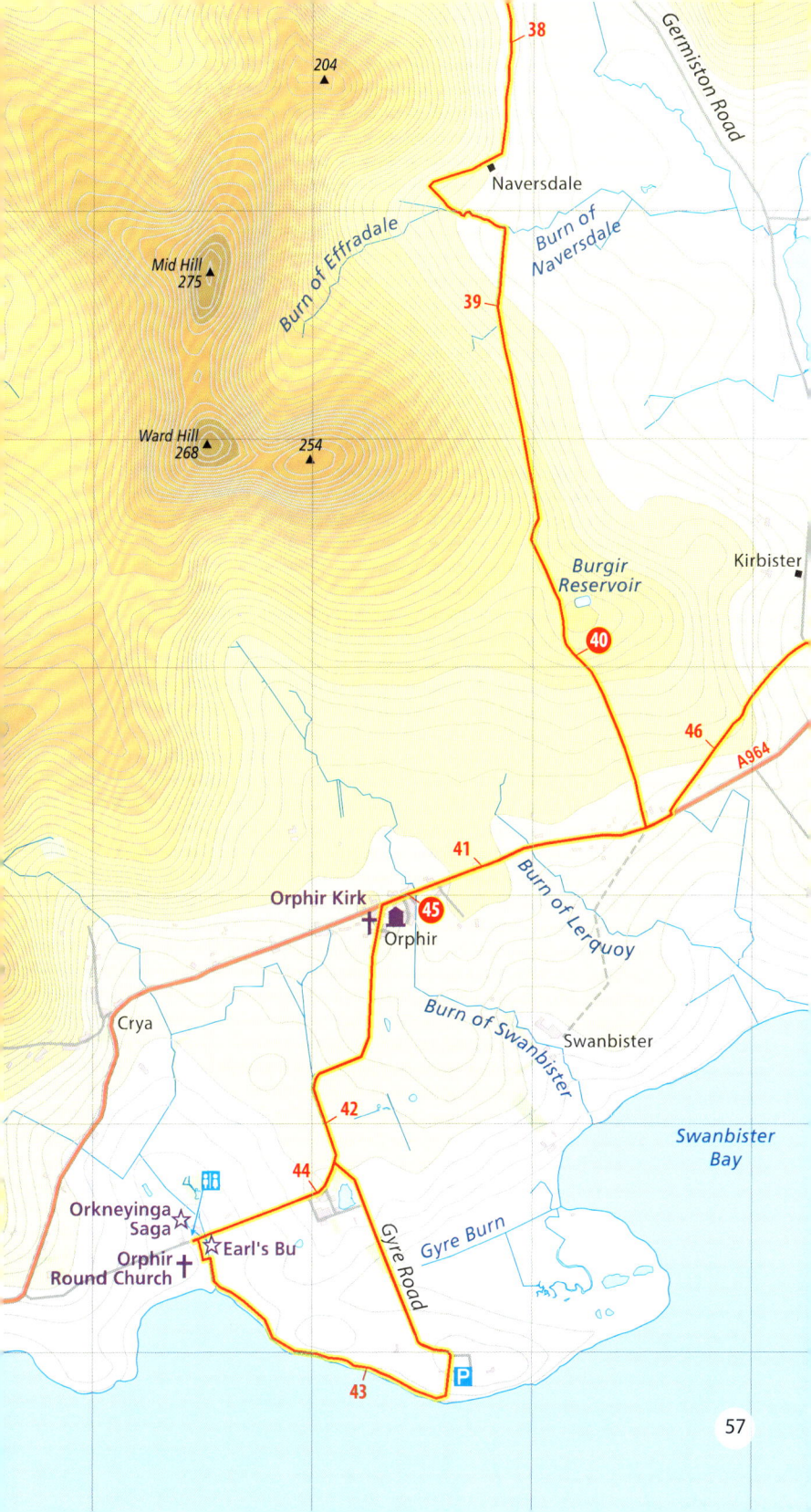

3·6 Orphir to Kirkwall

59	62	63

Distance 12·8 miles 20·6 km
Terrain largely offroad (67%), with a few km of pathless heather; the rest is minor road and pavement
Grade mostly low-level with some minor ascents
Food and drink none until Kirkwall
Summary a long, mainly coastal, section dominated by Scapa Flow seascapes, and culminating in the approach to St Magnus Cathedral

```
43·7      3·1    Mill Burn    3·1     Salt Pan      4·4      Royal Oak  2·2    56·5
Orphir     5·0              5·0                 7·1                 3·5   Kirkwall
```

- Start from the Orkneyinga Saga Centre by the car park. Walk east at first on the Gyre Road, which after bending left, right and left returns to Orphir village within 2·1 km.
- Pass Orphir Kirk on the left and meet the main road opposite the war memorial. Turn right onto its pavement heading east towards Kirkwall, retracing your steps at the end of 3·5.
- Note the track you came down from Burgir, opposite Symbister, and after another 130 m bear left up a signed track. Follow this grassy track gently uphill, then gently downhill where it becomes a gravel drive that joins a minor road (from Kirbister).
- Turn right for 300 m to join the A964 road opposite the Old Schoolhouse, at a bike shelter. Cross the Mill Burn and its pumping station, and various buildings on the left. About 300 m after the burn, look overhead for electricity cables across the road.
- Below them on the right, the waymarked gate leads to a path down to Waulkmill Bay (mile 47). Before taking it, know if you are heading for an extra high tide: see the panel on page 59.
- Otherwise follow the grassy path to the far end of the field and go through another gate to follow the potentially boggy path, sometimes vague but waymarked in places.
- Once you reach the shore, a waymarker points you left around Waulkmill Bay, a fine sandy beach facing south-east (mile 47·6).

Potentially boggy path

West over Waulkmill Bay

Extreme high tide
On occasion, an extreme high tide can flood the path to Waulkmill Bay, making it impassable. Rather than risk having to backtrack, find out ahead of time if this will affect you. See page 70 for a source of tidal predictions. To avoid the flooded path, continue beside the A964 for a further 1 km, then turn right down the minor road to Waulkmill Bay. This lets you rejoin the Way at mile 47·8: see map above.

- The path climbs up from the shore in a series of steps to join the road where you turn right, soon passing public toilets. Continue past a sign 'No vehicles beyond this point' to Sandygill. Turn left and soon cross a stile to follow a waymarked track up through the heather.
- Within 1 km the track reaches this grand tall stile with handrails. Cross the Burn of Vam at mile 48·7 and continue over a second, matching stile.
- ⚠ The path beyond becomes ill-defined. Ignore the tempting track uphill to the left and continue east through the heather on an indistinct route. Throughout this section, follow wooden posts, but only if they carry SMW waymarkers.
- After a short climb, three consecutive waymarker posts send you downhill towards the coast at Cony Geo, and navigation becomes simpler from here on.

Rocks near Cony Geo

Tall stile near Burn of Vam

Descent to Cony Geo

- Continue eastwards along a low cliff through bracken and heather, with fine views across Scapa Flow. The path runs parallel to the coast for the next 1 km. When you reach the corner of a low wire fence, continue on its seaward side.
- One km after Cony Geo, descend steeply to Salt Pan, a small bay. At the beach, cross the burn by a small wooden plank.
- Climb the short steep slope up from the beach and after a further 500 m reach a waymarker that turns you inland and uphill. Turn left **before** the first barbed-wire fence: don't try to walk between the two fences.

- The track leads uphill through heather for 1 km before a right-left dogleg at Coal Hill, then after a further 350 m it rejoins the A964 road.

Low cliffs on the approach to Scapa Bay

- Turn right along the main road for 1 km until you reach the sign to the Foveran Restaurant. Turn right down its access road.
- After 300 m pass to the right of the restaurant buildings. Afterwards, take a track that leads to the shore, bearing slightly right through the heather at its halfway point.
- Reach the shore at Hesti Geo: see page 63 for its photo. Turn left onto a narrow path that winds above the shore, with some exposure in places and some reassuring metal strips to protect its edges. Look ahead for your first inspiring glimpse of St Magnus Cathedral, and pass above the beach at Red Craig.
- The path continues its sinuous path around Scapa Bay, passing Scapa Distillery at mile 53·6. For tours and tastings, booking is essential: **www.scapawhisky.com** or phone 01856 873 269.

Cattle beside Scapa Distillery

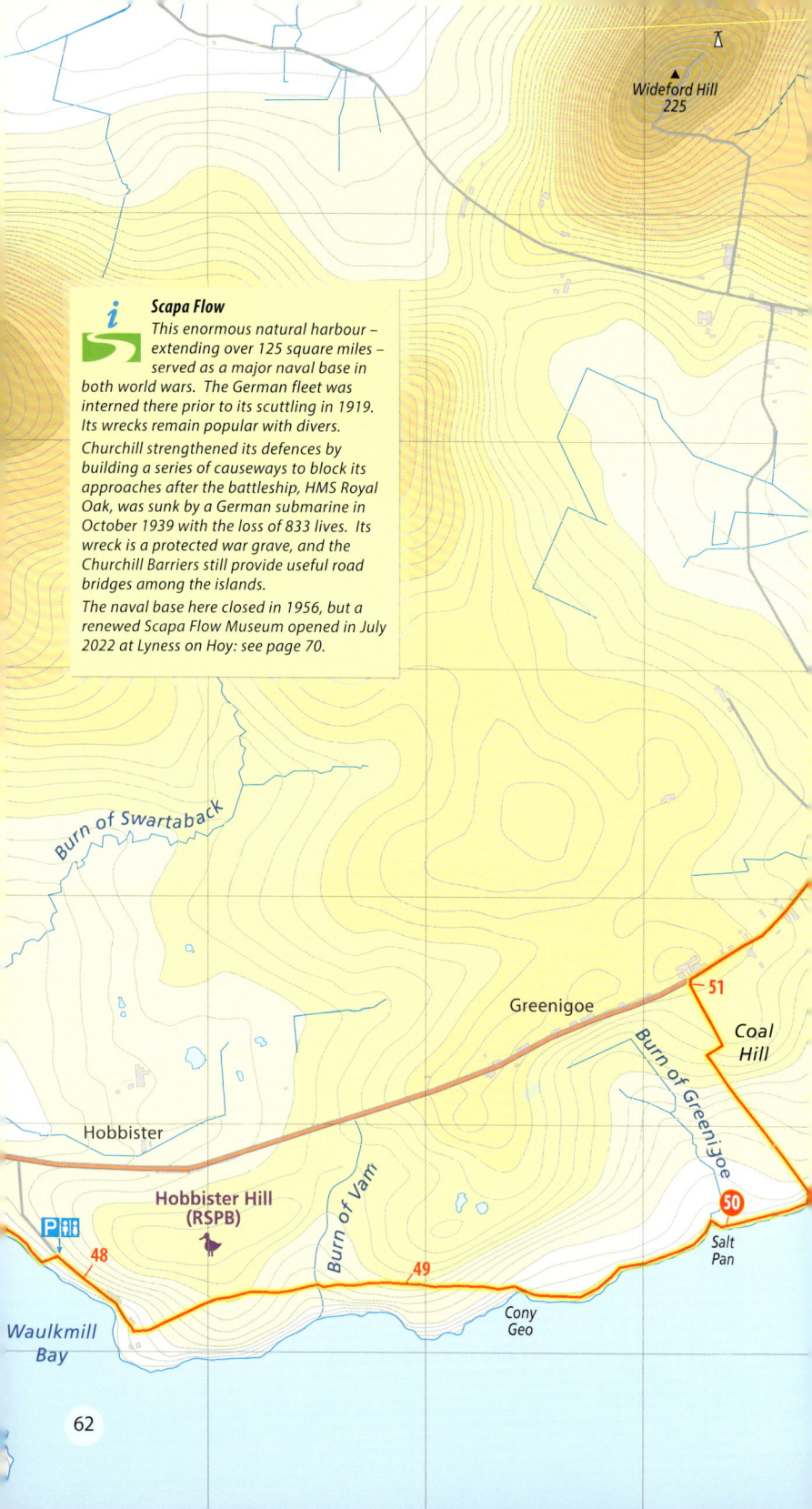

Scapa Flow

This enormous natural harbour – extending over 125 square miles – served as a major naval base in both world wars. The German fleet was interned there prior to its scuttling in 1919. Its wrecks remain popular with divers.

Churchill strengthened its defences by building a series of causeways to block its approaches after the battleship, HMS Royal Oak, was sunk by a German submarine in October 1939 with the loss of 833 lives. Its wreck is a protected war grave, and the Churchill Barriers still provide useful road bridges among the islands.

The naval base here closed in 1956, but a renewed Scapa Flow Museum opened in July 2022 at Lyness on Hoy: see page 70.

Hesti Geo

- The path continues to pass around most of Scapa Beach. Depending on the tide you may prefer to walk on the beach or along the road (B9053), heading for the bus stop beside the Royal Oak memorial gardens and display.
- Afterwards, turn left up the New Scapa Road (B9148) for 300 m to pick up the left turn signed for the Crantit Trail. At first it runs with the drainage ditch to its right, then after the Crantit Dairy access road, it changes sides. After a total of 1 km, make a right-left dogleg to resume briefly on New Scapa Road.
- Head north across the roundabout beside the Balfour Hospital and follow the pavement beside the A963 all the way to Kirkwall's harbour, now less than 1 mile away. En route you pass St Joseph's Church and the VisitScotland iCentre with bus station, with the spire of St Magnus tempting you to detour offroute to your right.
- However the Way turns right at the harbour and after 100 m turns right into Bridge Street. Just before its end, make a short detour left into St Olaf's Wynd to see the archway of St Olaf's Kirk.

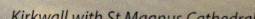

Obelisk memorial to HMS Royal Oak

Kirkwall with St Magnus Cathedral

- Retrace your steps afterwards to resume Bridge Street, very soon to turn right down Albert Street – paved but not pedestrianised. After it becomes Broad Street, the cathedral appears on the left.

- If you arrive outside its opening hours (see *www.stmagnus.org*) your pilgrimage now ends at the plaque with the St Magnus Way logo cast in bronze and set into the pavement.

- If the cathedral is open, you will want to linger in this magnificent building: see pages 21-2 and 66-7 for more. Be sure to visit the St Magnus Way Pilgrim's Table in the south transept where you can sign the Pilgrims' Logbook and ask for your completion certificate and scallop shell: donations appropriate. There are prayers relating to the themes and sections of the route on hand-held paddles.

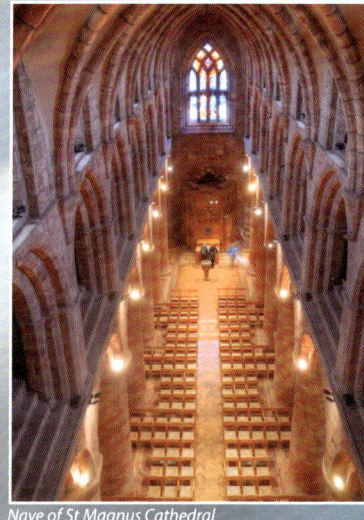
Nave of St Magnus Cathedral

Congratulations on completing St Magnus Way! Whatever your next pilgrimage, we hope that this one has been memorable.

Kirkwall

Kirkwall is the capital of Orkney, and home to nearly 40% of its population. To understand its importance, remember that roads are a relatively recent form of transport, and for much of history the sea was the main highway for trade, pilgrimage and warfare. The Norse seafaring empire saw Kirkwall as the hub of a network connecting Scandinavia with Shetland, Iceland, the Western Isles and parts of Ireland.

Kirkwall's harbour was crucial to trade, and the sea formerly extended deeper inland to include the Peedie Sea (now an inland lake). During the 18th century, there was a rich trade in kelp, a source of chemicals for the glass and soap industries. Since 1811 the harbour has been improved, with several extensions to the main pier. In 2003 the deep-water pier at Hatson was developed about two miles to the north-west. This serves Orkney's visiting cruise ships (about 150 per annum) as well as NorthLink Ferries. Conveniently for island-hopping, Orkney Ferries still use Kirkwall's town harbour, which is busy with fishing and leisure boats.

Kirkwall's name comes from old Norse meaning church bay, reflecting the foundation of St Olaf's in the early 11th century: the Way visits its arched doorway and plaque on page 64. The town was already a thriving centre for trade, and Earl Rognvald's foundation of a cathedral for his uncle, St Magnus, followed in 1137.

This glorious two-tone sandstone building marks the end of the St Magnus Way. Walkers who arrive during its opening hours can visit the Pilgrim's Table: see the photo opposite. To visit the cathedral properly, take your time and use its superb guidebook: see page 71. For its upper levels, book a guided tour via its website www.stmagnus.org. For a 15-minute video, visit the adjacent St Magnus Centre.

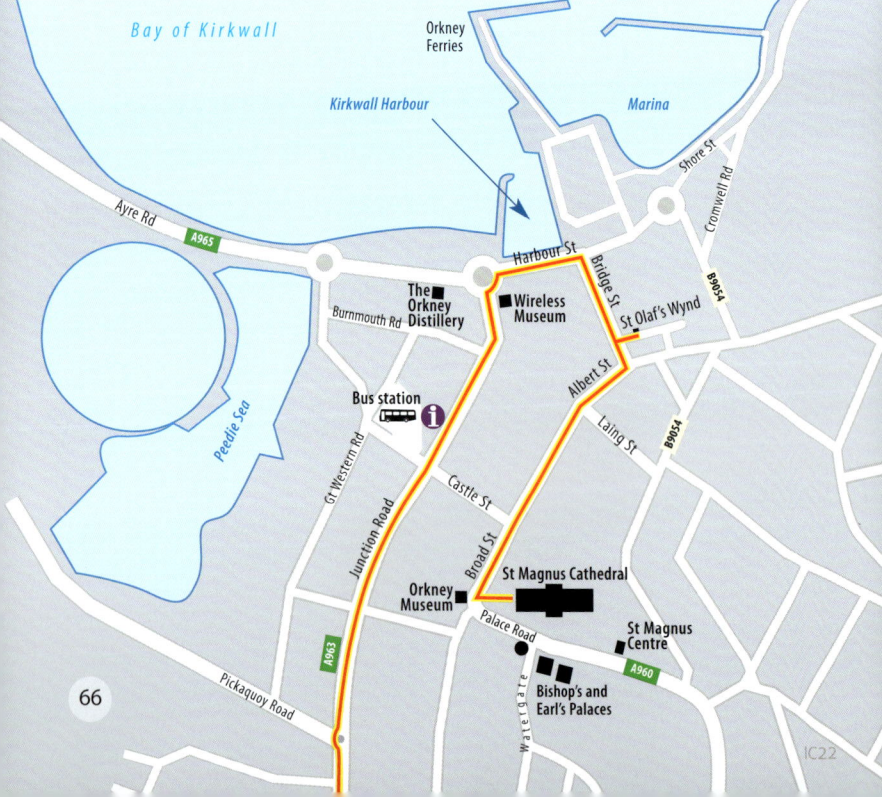

The nearby Orkney Museum offers extensive exhibits – Viking, medieval and modern – and is highly recommended: see page 70.

Around the corner from the cathedral is the massive circular tower of the Bishop's Palace. Originally built in the mid-12th century, this tower was added in the 1540s by Bishop Robert Reid, founder of Edinburgh University. His son Patrick later acquired adjacent land by crooked means and used slave labour to build the Earl's Palace in 1607 – the finest Renaissance building in Scotland.

The Pilgrim's Table, St Magnus Cathedral

Patrick was unable to enjoy it after he was imprisoned in 1610. Then in 1614 his son Robert seized the palace, cathedral and nearby castle. The castle was destroyed in the ensuing siege and father and son were executed. The surviving buildings are partly ruined but well worth a visit: see **bit.ly/SMW-earls**. The top of the round tower offers a splendid view of the cathedral.

The Orkney Wireless Museum was founded in 1983 by Jim MacDonald, a collector and historian of wireless communications in Orkney and further afield. It houses a fascinating set of military and domestic equipment, from radar and radios to juke boxes and novelty transistor radios: see page 70. There are three distilleries here and nearby: Highland Park and Scapa (malt whisky) and Orkney Distillery (gin, opened in 2018). See page 70 (*Other useful links*) for visit details.

Kirkwall has an interesting range of specialised shops, welcoming pubs and fine dining. It's wise to book ahead, because restaurants fill up quickly, especially at weekends and in season. Visit the iCentre to collect a free map and leaflets, including the splendid *Kirkjuvagr* booklet – a pocket guide to Kirkwall's history with town walks of various lengths.

Earl's Palace, Kirkwall

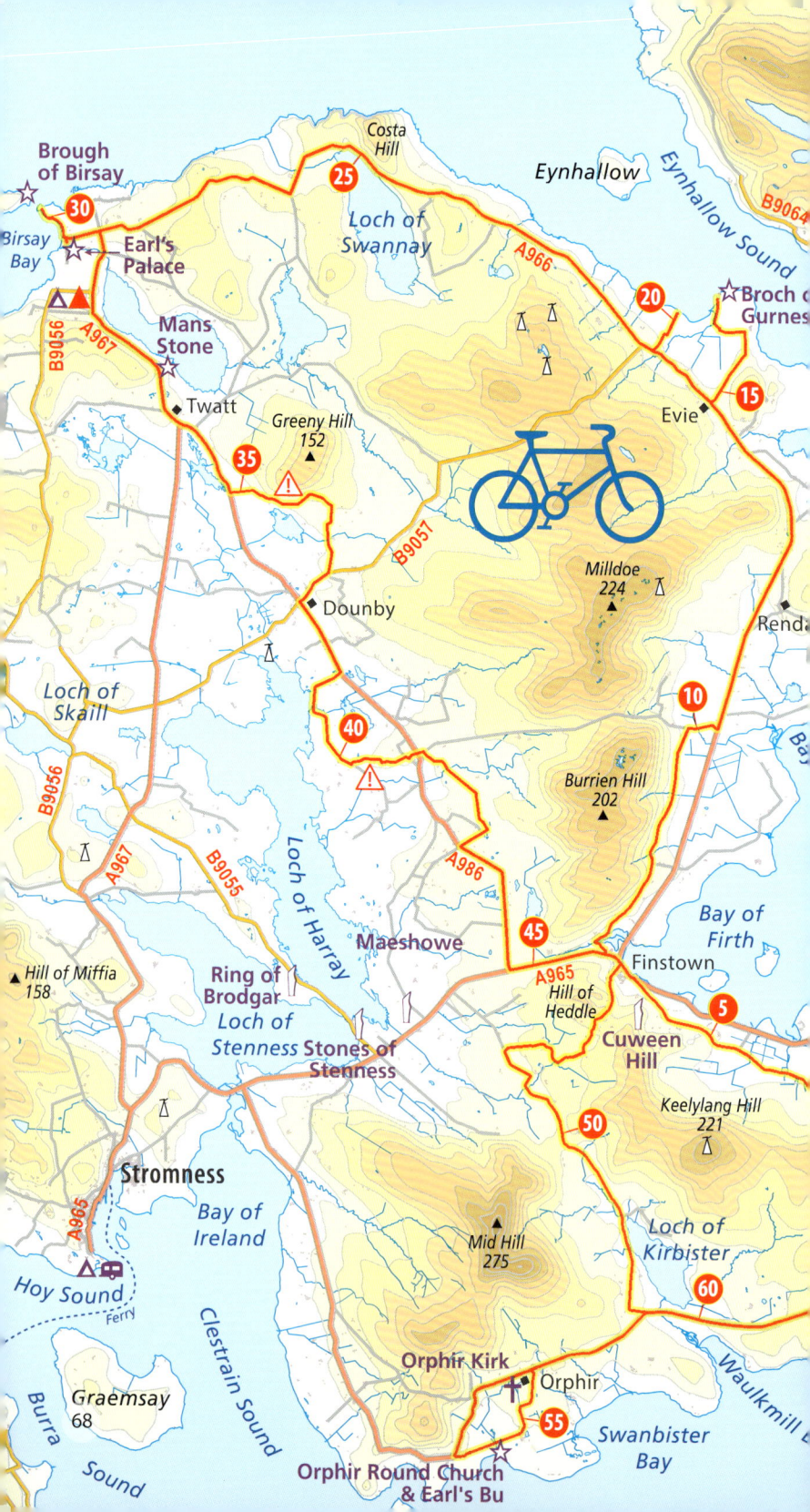

4 St Magnus Cycleway

This 67-mile cycleway follows tarmac roads almost throughout: see this web page for more information, links to advice for cyclists and animations of various options: *bit.ly/SM-cycle*.

Experienced, fit cyclists may complete it in a single day; others will enjoy it in a more leisurely fashion as either or both of two circuits: a 27-mile southern loop from Kirkwall and/or a 40-mile northern circuit from Finstown.

For the two shorter circuits, any kind of bike could be suitable, but if attempting the full 67 miles in one day you need a road or touring bike. You might need to dismount in wet conditions for two very short offroad sections shown here with warning triangles near Dounby. If wanting to bring your own bike to Orkney, check page 71 for ferry operator conditions.

Our map shows cumulative mileage from Kirkwall following the direction suggested by the website. However the route is not waymarked and can be ridden in the reverse direction.

5 Reference

Creation of St Magnus Way

The life and cult of St Magnus led to a tradition of medieval pilgrimages to Orkney. This in turn inspired the group Orkney Pilgrimage to create a modern walking route. In 2016 the group set itself the ambitious goal of launching this route for the 900th anniversary of St Magnus' death. The project's success relied on the, drive, determination and inspiration of David McNeish, former Church of Scotland Minister at the Milestone Community Church in Dounby, Dr Sarah Jane Gibbon of the University of the Highlands and Islands and the other Orkney Pilgrimage trustees. The Way's official website is at
   www.stmagnusway.com and it includes a link to the dedicated app, as well as many historical and cultural resources. In particular it has notes and reflective questions on the Way's six themes: see page 5 and
   bit.ly/SMW-resources.

Cathedral and museums

In Kirkwall, the star attraction is St Magnus Cathedral, but be sure also to visit the adjacent St Magnus Centre with its excellent 15-minute video. Details of both are at
   www.stmagnus.org
Also in Kirkwall, visit the outstanding Orkney Museum
   bit.ly/SMW-museum and, near the harbour, the Orkney Wireless Museum:
   bit.ly/SMW-wireless
The Kirbuster Farm Museum (tel 01856 771 268) is an 800 m diversion off the St Magnus Way (see page 43) and well worth a visit. Check its opening times:
   bit.ly/SMW-kirbuster
The Scapa Flow Museum on Hoy is devoted to Orkney's military role in World Wars 1 and 2, and opened in July 2022:
   bit.ly/SMW-scapa

Weather forecasts

Forecasts for up to ten days ahead can be found at
   www.metoffice.gov.uk
   www.bbc.co.uk/weather

Tides

The best general source of advance information about tides in Scotland is
   tides4fishing.com/uk/scotland then scroll down (or search) for various Orkney tidal ports.
For specific information about Birsay Bay, but only for the week ahead, visit this page from *tideschart.com*:
   bit.ly/SMW-birsay
Beware of relying on general predictions because Orkney's geography means that within the archipelago tidal highs and lows can vary by up to an hour.

Maps (printed and online) and GPX

Ordnance Survey shows the whole of West Mainland on its Explorer sheet 463, but its scale (1:25,000) is only slightly better than the mapping in this book. In its current edition (last revised 2018) the line of St Magnus Way is not shown at all. Sheet 463 omits the last two miles into Kirkwall. For visitors, the Landranger (1:50,000) may be more useful: sheet 6 shows the entire Mainland and inner islands including Egilsay.

For a very detailed online route map, click the map graphic on this page
   www.rucsacs.com/books/smw
and zoom in repeatedly. The page also offers a GPX download (under Bonus content).

Accommodation

Accommodation, especially for single nights, can be difficult to find even when booking long in advance. Here are two recommended sites:
   bit.ly/SMW-accomm
   www.orkney.com/plan/accommodation
but try also general sources such as Google maps and
   airbnb.co.uk

Other useful links

For a wide range of websites useful for this route, visit
   rucsacs.com/route-links/st-magnus-way

John Rae Society

The society is dedicated to celebrating Rae's achievements and preserving his heritage, including Hall of Clestrain where he was born:
   www.johnraesociety.com

Travel and transport
Flights
Loganair operates flights to Kirkwall (KOI) from Glasgow, Edinburgh, Inverness and Aberdeen with onward connections to Belfast, Cardiff, Dublin, Manchester and other destinations:
www.loganair.co.uk
Bus route 4 takes you from the airport to Kirkwall in ten minutes and runs every 30 minutes on weekdays, with times more restricted at weekends.

Ferries
Ferry routes from the Scottish mainland
To reach a ferry terminal on the Scottish mainland by train means reaching rail stations at Aberdeen or Thurso (two miles from Scrabster): visit
www.scotrail.co.uk
NorthLink Ferries operates both Aberdeen/Kirkwall and Scrabster/Stromness. The Aberdeen route takes six to seven hours with three sailings per week in summer and two in winter. NorthLink's Scrabster route takes only 90 minutes and plies 2-3 times a day, seven days a week. Visit
www.northlinkferries.co.uk for current timetables, check-in and prices.

Pentland Ferries offers a one-hour crossing between Gills Bay, near John o' Groats, and St Margaret's Hope in South Ronaldsay, 3 or 4 times a day:
www.pentlandferries.co.uk
The above are vehicle ferries all of which take bikes free of charge, though NorthLink asks you to book the bike. For pedestrians and cyclists there was also (May to September 2022) a twice-daily 40-minute sea crossing from John O'Groats to Burwick, with a connecting bus to Kirkwall:
www.jogferry.co.uk

Ferries within Orkney
For the ferry Tingwall/Egilsay, visit
www.orkneyferries.co.uk and select Rousay, Egilsay & Wyre – a circular route that includes two other islands. Be sure to book your return journey which is on request only. Bikes travel free and don't need to be booked.

For Hoy (see page 24) passengers can use the Stromness/Moaness ferry but if taking a vehicle use the Houton (near Orphir) to Lyness service. Bikes travel free and don't need to be booked.

Buses
For buses within Orkney, visit
www.stagecoachbus.com or the Council website at
bit.ly/SMW-bus or pick up a timetable from the bus station in Kirkwall. Aside from central Kirkwall and Stromness, you can hail a bus anywhere on its route that is safe for a bus to stop.

Notes for novices
If you are new to long-distance walking, read our advice on daily distances, foot care and equipment: visit
bit.ly/RR-novices

Further reading
Orkneyinga Saga (1981) translated by Herman Palsson and Paul Edwards, Penguin Classics 978-0-140-44383-7.
St Magnus Cathedral (2007) Jarrold publishing 978-0-7117-4467-7 28pp, on sale in the cathedral at £3.

Acknowledgements
The author thanks all the Trustees, notably Stuart Little and Caroline Butterfield.

Photo credits
We thank these photographers for their images: Colin Keldie front cover, 41l, 50l, 51l; Iain Knox 37, 38l, 46l, 51u, 52, 54u, 54-5; Stuart Little 63; Michael Maggs 17u; David Mazza 23u, 41u, 42u, 58l; Fionn McArthur/*startpointmedia.co.uk* 4-5, 8, 15, 24-5, 43u; Jacquetta Megarry 10, 12 (8 of 9), 13 (all 9), 14, 18, 22u, 25l, 26l, 27m, 32m, 34u, 34l, 38u, 40, 43m, 46u, 47, 54m, 55u, 55m, 58u, 60 (all 3), 64u, 67u; Dawn Moody 22l, 30, 32l, 36, 44u, 44l, 50u, 56u, 61l, 64-65; John Mottram/*istockphoto.com* 25u; *northernvicar.co.uk* 21, 48u, 48l; Tom O'Brien 32u; Frances Pelly 35; Society of the Friends of St Magnus Cathedral 20.

We thank also *dreamstime.com* and photographers for these images: Creativehearts title page, Geoff Eccles 16u, Leon Wilhelm 16m, Bobbrooky 16-17, Jeremy Brown 19u, Rob Atherton 19l, Wojciech Kruczynski 23l, David Woods 24u, Beth Baisch 26u, Lukas Blazek 26m, Brian Kushner 27u and 28u, Ansar Kyzylaliyeu 27l, Jamesahanlon 28l, Michael Schroeder 29u, Villehardouin 29l, David Lloyd 33, Harold Stiver 39u, Rphstock 39l, Alfiofer 56l, Alan5766 65u, Juliane Jacobs 67l.

Index

A
accommodation 9, 70

B
Barony Mill 16, 41
Binscarth Woods 24, 25, 49, 51
Birsay 8, 9, 10, 18, 21, 40, 41, 42
Brough of Birsay 11, 27, 39
bus services 10, 71

C
camping 9, 10, 15
Cuween Hill, Chambered Cairn 52, 54
cycling, cycleway 9, 68-69, 71

D
distances and time needed 8-9
diver, red-throated 29
dogs and livestock 14
dolphin, Risso's 26
Dounby 8, 9, 10, 44, 46
duck, eider 26
duck, pintail 29

E
Earl's Palace, Birsay 40, 41
Egilsay 5, 8, 9, 20, 21, 30-32, 71

F
ferries 11, 24, 30, 66, 71
Finstown 8, 9, 10, 51, 52, 69

G
geology and scenery 23-24
geos 7, 13, 23, 24, 32, 38, 39, 60, 61, 63
Gurness, Broch of 17, 33

H
habitats and wildlife 25-29
Heart of Neolithic Orkney WHS 6, 16
history 6-7, 16-19

K
Kirbuster Farm Museum 43, 70
Kirkwall 6, 8, 9, 10, 11, 18, 21, 64-5, 66-7, 70, 71

M
Mans Stones 21, 43
Mans Well 41

N
Naversdale 55
navigation and waymarking 12
neolithic Orkney 6, 16
Norse rule, Norn language 7, 16-18, 66
Northern marsh orchid 25
Notes for novices 9, 71

O
Orkney, as a destination 6-7
Orkney Museum 67, 70
Orkney vole 25, 28
Orphir 8, 9, 55, 56, 58
owl, short-eared 28

P
packing checklist 15
peregrine falcon 27
puffin 27

R
Rae, John 18, 19, 22, 70
road-walking 9, 13

S
Scapa Flow, museum 6, 19, 23, 26, 44, 54, 62, 70
Scottish Outdoor Access Code 14
Scottish primrose 27
seals, grey and common 26
St Magnus 5, 18, 20-22, 66
St Magnus Cathedral 5, 18, 21, 22, 65, 66, 67, 70
St Magnus Church
 - Birsay 18, 21, 40, 41
 - Egilsay 4, 31-33
stoat 25

T
terrain 12-13
themes (of the Way) 5, 65, 70
tides 11, 34, 39, 59, 70
transport and travel 10, 11, 71

W
waymarking 12
waystones 34, 35
weather 8, 70
wildlife 25-29
World Wars 1 and 2 19, 23, 62